'An excellent resource to guide every new teacher th[rough]
education.'
— **Kevin Hogston**, *Head Teacher at*

'I wish I had this book to hand when I was a newly qualified teacher! It offers such sage and practical advice for everything a new teacher may encounter when starting in their new role.'
— **Sue Jakob**, *Deputy Head & School Based Mentor for ITT students*

'This is a must-read for all new teachers entering the teaching profession. Exploring the demands of teaching from personal experience and the experiences of many trainee teachers, Bron's love of teaching shines through on every page.'
— **Rachel Leventhall**, *Educational Consultant*

Being a Primary Teacher

Being a Primary Teacher provides key advice on preparing for and undertaking final placements, securing the first teaching post and getting ready for the first class, through to the first year of teaching. Throughout the book, Bronwen Cullum draws on her years of experience teaching in primary schools and in a university working with trainee teachers to provide guidance and support for teachers.

Divided into three parts, the book explores the various challenges that those learning to be teachers face in the early stages of their career. It includes numerous practical examples, useful resources and templates as well as check lists at the end of each chapter. The chapters explore essential topics including:

- applying for a job and preparing for interviews;
- building and managing relationships in the classroom and with staff;
- the transition from training to the first job as a primary school teacher;
- preparation for the progress of children;
- looking after yourself.

This book is an essential read for trainees and newly qualified teachers wanting to enhance their professional development and maximise their potential so that they can fully enjoy the profession of teaching.

Bronwen Cullum is a former primary teacher and university lecturer. She was the Deputy Director for Primary and Early Years at Kingston University London, UK.

Being a Primary Teacher

Moving from Trainee to NQT

Bronwen Cullum

Routledge
Taylor & Francis Group
LONDON AND NEW YORK

First published 2020
by Routledge
2 Park Square, Milton Park, Abingdon, Oxon OX14 4RN

and by Routledge
52 Vanderbilt Avenue, New York, NY 10017

Routledge is an imprint of the Taylor & Francis Group, an informa business

© 2020 Bronwen Cullum

The right of Bronwen Cullum to be identified as author of this work has been asserted by her in accordance with sections 77 and 78 of the Copyright, Designs and Patents Act 1988.

All rights reserved. No part of this book may be reprinted or reproduced or utilised in any form or by any electronic, mechanical, or other means, now known or hereafter invented, including photocopying and recording, or in any information storage or retrieval system, without permission in writing from the publishers.

Trademark notice: Product or corporate names may be trademarks or registered trademarks, and are used only for identification and explanation without intent to infringe.

British Library Cataloguing-in-Publication Data
A catalogue record for this book is available from the British Library

Library of Congress Cataloging-in-Publication Data
Names: Cullum, Bronwen, author.
Title: Being a primary teacher : moving from trainee to NQT / Bronwen Cullum.
Description: Abingdon, Oxon ; New York : Routledge, 2020.
Identifiers: LCCN 2019050044 (print) | LCCN 2019050045 (ebook) |
ISBN 9780367278885 (hardback) | ISBN 9780367278892 (paperback) |
ISBN 9780429298561 (ebook)
Subjects: LCSH: Primary school teaching. | Primary school teachers. |
First year teachers. | Education, Primary. | Effective teaching.
Classification: LCC LB1555 .C85 2020 (print) |
LCC LB1555 (ebook) | DDC 372.11–dc23
LC record available at https://lccn.loc.gov/2019050044
LC ebook record available at https://lccn.loc.gov/2019050045

ISBN: 978-0-367-27888-5 (hbk)
ISBN: 978-0-367-27889-2 (pbk)
ISBN: 978-0-429-29856-1 (ebk)

Typeset in Bembo and Helvetica Neue
by Newgen Publishing UK

This book is dedicated to all the inspirational teachers, lecturers and trainee teachers with whom I have had the privilege to work with over the years.

You will never know the full extent of the difference you make to the lives of others.

Contents

Introduction — 1

PART 1 Applying for your first job and final school placement — 3

1 Applying for a job and the interview — 5

2 Getting ready for the final placement — 18

3 Managing relationships — 30

4 Thorough preparation — 39

5 Knowing the children and pupil progress — 49

PART 2 The transition phase: the transition from training to your first job as a primary school teacher — 61

6 Building upon and developing new relationships — 63

7 Getting to know your future class — 72

8 The classroom as an empty box: where do I start? — 82

9 Planning — 92

PART 3 The first year of teaching — 105

10 Building relationships and community in the classroom — 107

11 Preparation and planning for the progress of children — 116

12 Language and learning	123
13 Building professional relationships	136
14 Looking after yourself	148

Introduction

This book is written after having spent years teaching in primary schools and in a university working with trainee teachers. I use the word 'trainee' guardedly as my last intention is to actually train someone, but for ease of language, bearing in mind all the different settings in which people learn to be teachers, the term trainee is used in this book. I hope everyone on their journey in the teaching profession embraces learning in order to help make informed decisions based on the context in which they find themselves. Also because of the different routes into teaching I use the term 'final placement' throughout the book as a name for the final assessed placement trainee teachers undertake in school before becoming a qualified teacher.

This book is primarily for anyone learning how to become a teacher as well as those who are newly qualified. It is also a book that has the potential to be used by mentors. It is a reminder of the different challenges that those learning to be teachers face in the early stages of their career with practical examples that have the potential to be used in mentor meetings.

So why did I write this book?

At university I have worked with trainee teachers preparing them for their final placement and in schools I have helped newly qualified teachers in the summer holidays preparing for their first class and indeed mentored those in their first year of teaching and beyond. I have witnessed the challenges that are encountered at each stage and wanted to help with key advice for each stage. I also wanted to make strong links between 'training' and becoming qualified and the flow into the first year of teaching.

The amount of information that trainee teachers and newly qualified teachers receive is sometimes overwhelming. I have lectured trainee teachers about pedagogical understanding, such as: behaviour, beliefs and values, well-being, professionalism, planning, learning theories, assessment, special needs and disabilities. All of this learning is key to understanding the foundations of knowledge that all teachers should receive but how does this transfer to applying for a job, the final placement of a trainee teacher, the setting up of a classroom, and the first year of teaching? The book explores the key elements of practice to focus on at these stages. The aim is not to overwhelm the reader but to give succinct practical advice.

Ultimately I wanted this book to help trainee and newly qualified teachers to be successful in the early stages of their career with some key information based on my experiences and the experience of many others that has been sought whilst researching for and writing this book. You will not find any current educational strategies mentioned in this book; they come and go. The key elements of what makes an effective teacher mainly stay the same.

This book should therefore hopefully have longevity. Return to it occasionally to help keep you grounded.

Bronwen Cullum

PART 1
Applying for your first job and final school placement

CHAPTER 1

Applying for a job and the interview

This chapter should help you to:

- think carefully about the jobs you apply for;
- understand the importance of the initial visit to the school;
- prepare for letters of application for your first teaching post;
- prepare for an interview;
- think about key elements to include in an observed lesson;
- be aware of your digital footprint in preparation for an interview;
- be prepared when finding out whether you have got the job.

Introduction

This chapter aims to help you prepare as much as possible in advance of starting the final placement so that if job opportunities arise during placement, you know you will have put in the groundwork. It would be a shame to miss out on a job opportunity because you have not got the time whilst on placement to prepare. Of course, job opportunities can often arise before trainee teachers have even started their final school placement and this is the reason that this chapter is situated at the beginning of the book. If you do find yourself applying for a job before final placement, do read through the chapters in the first part of the book as they should help you prepare for the interview by highlighting key aspects of practice that you will need to draw on.

Thinking carefully about the jobs you apply for

It is really easy to feel as though you should apply for just about every job going in the area in which you want to teach for fear of not getting a job. In addition, it can seem a worry when other trainee teachers are getting jobs and you have not got one yet but it is really important that you apply for a job that suits you, both in terms of the age range you want to teach as well as the type of school you wish to teach in. Think of all the factors that make schools different and think about what potentially is right for you. If, for example, you apply for a single form entry school, you will not have the support of planning with others but you might relish the thought of the freedom of planning by yourself.

The values that schools hold should be evident on their web site. Have a look and think about whether you hold the same values and whether you feel comfortable promoting the school's values. This is particularly important when applying for a job in a faith school if you do not believe in the particular faith of the school. This is something that can always be explored with the headteacher. Many teachers who do not believe in the faith of the school in which they teach do successfully integrate into the ethos of the school. Only you will know whether you will feel comfortable with the expectations of the school, so do explore what these are.

The most current Ofsted report should also be on the school web site. Do not just look at the grade of the report but look at the content. The school may not have received a grade of 'good' because of an area of concern in a particular Key Stage, whilst the job opportunity is in a Key Stage where the practice is at least good. If the school has areas of concern, they may be looking for competent newly qualified teachers who can help turn the school around and there may be many new staff starting at the school, including new leadership. If it is a school that you are really interested in but you are concerned about the Ofsted report, do ring the school and ask to speak to the headteacher.

If the job is advertised as a vacancy for a primary teacher and you particularly want to work with a particular Key Stage, ring up and ask the headteacher which year group the job is for. There can potentially be quite a bit of movement of staff in a school at the end of the academic year with teachers retiring or getting new jobs so do make sure you will be working in an age range of your preference.

When applying for jobs you also need to think about the location of the school. If it is in the area in which you live, you need to be aware that you are highly likely to meet children and their parents/carers at weekends and in the evenings. Some teachers are fine with this and like being part of the local community whilst others like to have a little space between their work place and their home. Equally you need to consider the amount of time you are prepared to travel to and from work. The importance of a work/life balance is really crucial, so this is something that you will need to consider carefully.

The initial visit to the school

This visit cannot be underestimated and must be treated as part of the interview process. It is really important that you do try to visit the school and it is best to do this before writing the letter of application. You are looking to see if the school is right for you, so you do not want to waste time writing a letter of application that you will not use. It is always best to visit during the school day so that you can get a real feel for the school. Visiting during school hours may not always be possible when you are on your final placement; if this is the case then you may have to visit after school hours. Before the visit you should have looked at the school web site to glean as much information as possible about the school. Try to find out something that is special about the school; maybe they promote a creative curriculum or maybe their sports teams are really successful. Make sure you have something positive to say about the school when you visit to demonstrate your knowledge and interest in the school.

Dress for the visit as if you are going for an interview. First impressions are really important. Always shake hands when you are introduced to someone and smile. If you are in a group with other potential candidates you need to make sure you present yourself as confident and make sure you demonstrate that you are interested in what you are being shown. Ask questions and make comments on things you see, for instance, a lovely display. However, just be careful that you are not speaking too much: it is a fine balance between being interested and not being too vocal.

Whenever I have shown candidates around a school, I have been interested in how they interact with children in the classes. I may stop and spend a little longer in 1 class. Here I would be looking at what the candidates do. It is always a good sign when candidates get down to the level of the children and ask them about what they are learning. Get involved and do not hang back. Thank the teacher when you leave the classroom as well as any other adults who are in the classroom: this will demonstrate that you are polite and acknowledge that the teaching and learning has been interrupted. In every school I have worked in, the staff are asked about what they thought of the candidates so every person you meet on this visit is important. You are also deciding whether this is the right environment for you to work in. Schools can be very different in the ways in which they present themselves. Some schools are very business-like whilst others present as more of a family atmosphere. Which type of atmosphere will you feel more comfortable in?

Letter of application (sometimes called a personal statement or covering letter)

There are different ways to write a letter of application but all letters of application must have the following key elements.

Every letter must:

- be spelt correctly;
- have excellent grammar;
- demonstrate that you know the school that you are applying to.

Some job specifications may set out the criteria required for the job. If this is the case, use these as your guidelines. If there are many criteria, try to join up ideas in 1 paragraph (see examples in this chapter). If you know the school you are applying to has a specific intake, for example a high percentage of learners for whom English is an additional language, you must acknowledge and address this in the letter of application. You cannot fit everything into a letter of application so do not try to; make sensible choices based on the job specification and school.

You cannot write 1 letter of application and use this 1 letter to apply for all jobs. Rather than gear the whole letter to each school you apply to, alter the opening paragraph to immediately demonstrate to the reader that you have visited the school or that you know things that are special about the school from reading the school's web site.

Example 1—Opening paragraph

Thank you for allowing me to visit your school on Monday last week. I really appreciate the time taken to show me around. I was particularly fascinated in how the outdoor environment was being used to encourage the learning of phonics, as well as the different ways in which reluctant writers were being enticed to write. I notice this is a key target for the Year 1 cohort and am really interested in this as an English specialist. The focus on different ways to engage children in their learning that I observed in your school is something that I am really drawn to and would love to be part of the team planning for such learning opportunities.

Example 2—Opening paragraph

I am really interested in applying for a job at Lawn Primary School. I am aware of the school's excellent reputation for sport and have read about some of their successes in local newspapers as well as on your web site. As a keen sportswoman, in time I would love to help to continue and perhaps even build on the school's success in this area. I am also aware of how sport can be used in different aspects of the curriculum. In my last placement I successfully linked the teaching of athletics to Mathematics, ICT and PHSE. This was a fantastic motivational factor in getting the children to improve on their personal running times, jumps and throws. The children put their scores and times onto spread sheets in an ICT lesson. The analysis of the 'real life' data was used when teaching statistics. In PHSE the idea of working as a team was explored in detail.

These examples demonstrate how the candidates know something about the schools to which they are applying. Notice how example 2 uses the name of the school. This is particularly important if you are unable to actually visit the school prior to submitting the letter of application. Both examples also demonstrate how the candidates can potentially use their skills, knowledge, and understanding to contribute to the school.

The main body of the letter can then be used for most letters of application. If you know you want to work in a particular Key Stage then gear the writing to that Key Stage. The main body of the letter of application tends to be more meaningful if you draw on examples from your previous experiences.

Example 1—Paragraph within the body of the letter

On my last placement I was particularly pleased with how I developed my understanding of assessment for learning and how it became a key feature of most of my lessons. I understand the potential impact assessment for learning can have on the progress of children's learning, so I knew it was an important aspect of practice to develop. Getting the children to use the success criteria when reflecting on learning was particularly successful as was the use of peer marking. The evidence I collected to demonstrate progress in story writing using both these methods was commented on by my class teacher and mentor. This evidence of progress is evidenced in my portfolio which I would welcome the opportunity to show you if called for interview. I am currently developing my understanding of progress data and how this has the potential to inform pedagogical and organisational choices.

Example 2—Paragraph within the body of the letter

My understanding of the term behaviour for learning has increased significantly. By reflecting on lessons that have gone particularly well I have developed my understanding that meeting the needs of all learners through motivating, challenging and purposeful learning activities is crucial to behaviour. After meeting with the inclusion manager at my last placement I began to understand the needs of one particular child. In most lessons the child had only written the date after 10 minutes and then she would start to distract other children. I learnt the child could not retain multiple instructions. Understanding her needs helped me to adapt my teaching so the child could access learning. Drawing on the expertise of this member of staff really helped me understand that behaviour for learning is also about knowing the learning needs of every child. I also learnt about the importance of learning from the expertise of other teachers.

Both of these examples demonstrate key understanding of pedagogical issues in practice. Example 1 includes an understanding of the importance of pupil progress. This is important to get into a letter of application as headteachers and governors who are likely to be interviewing you will have a keen interest in your understanding of the progress of children's learning. If you are applying for a job prior to your final placement you may not have vast knowledge of progress data but the final sentence demonstrates that you have some understanding. You should be able to expand on this statement in an interview.

Example 2 demonstrates your understanding of behaviour for learning as well as meeting the special needs of a particular child. A key element of this example is demonstrating that you are not afraid to seek help, that you recognise the expertise of the teachers in the school, and that you act on advice. Presenting yourself as open to continually being a learner is important to get in a letter of application.

The letter of application is usually no longer than 2 pages and should include:

- an opening paragraph demonstrating you know the school you are applying to;
- behaviour and behaviour for learning;
- knowing the children as learners and understanding the process of learning;
- progress and attainment (AfL, pupil progress, and attainment data);
- the importance of positive working relationships (teachers, TAs, LSAs, parents/carers, mentor);
- a final paragraph that says something about your interests and what you can bring to the school and your attitude as a life-long learner.

Demonstrate your understanding of key issues with rich examples where possible. Try also to use current educational 'buzz' words.

The final paragraph needs to be punchy. The reader will want to know about you as a person and what you can bring to the school.

Example 1—Final paragraph

This letter of application highlights some key elements of teaching and learning that I believe are significant to being a successful primary school teacher. I understand that there is so much to learn and I am someone who enjoys and relishes the constant challenges that one faces in teaching. I understand the importance of my role as a mentee and also the important role that mentors play in developing newly qualified teachers.

Through my position as a student representative this academic year, I understand the need to be professional at all times. This role has enabled me to work with and liaise with many different people and I believe this will stand me in good stead for the different people teachers need to work with in the community of school. A phrase that has been used to describe me on my last placement was, 'a real team player'. I would hope to bring this attribute to your school.

I would welcome the opportunity to expand on any of the points I have raised in this letter and if successful would welcome the opportunity to be part of the team at Westfields Primary School.

Example 2—Final paragraph

I believe that it is really important to have your own personal interests and my key interests are running and reading. I know that these hobbies have helped me as a trainee teacher. Running has taught me about the importance of resilience and to keep going! In running you can always go faster; in teaching you can always learn more.

I love getting lost in a good book and have really developed an interest in children's literature. I believe this enthusiasm can be contagious and I relish the challenge of trying to hook children into reading a wide range of genres.

I would welcome an opportunity to expand on any of the points I have raised in this letter of application in an interview. I have a portfolio of children's learning that includes a cross curricular project I planned and taught on my last placement that I would love to share with you. If successful I feel confident that I have much to contribute to the school as well as learning from the experienced staff at Westfields Infants School.

Preparing for an interview

Preparation is the key word here. Reading the first part of this book should help you to prepare for most of the questions you are likely to be asked in an interview but you must be able to provide examples from your practice. Write out some examples where you can demonstrate how you have:

- taught your best lesson (what were the key elements?);
- taught your worst lesson (what did you learn from this?);
- evidenced progress of children's learning;
- met the needs of a child who has a special need;
- managed a child who presents with challenging behaviour:
- challenged a child who is achieving above age related expectations;
- acknowledged through planning and teaching the multi-cultural society in which we live;
- met the needs of learners for whom English is an additional language;
- incorporated some of your ideas into curriculum planning;
- worked successfully as a team member;
- contributed to the wider life of school;
- understood the current Safeguarding legislation and school procedures.

Taking a portfolio of evidence into the interview can really help you because the portfolio will jog your memory when you look at your best lesson plan from the last placement or if you can actually use some children's work to demonstrate evidence of children's learning. The portfolio does not have to be time consuming to put together. After your last placement just collate some pieces of evidence. Taking this in to the interview should ease your mind if you are at all worried about suddenly going blank. If you have not experienced all of the previous bullet points, engage in some research, for example, how you might meet the need of a child who presents with challenging behaviour. You should also research the school's web site, taking particular notice of value, vision, or mission statements, the curriculum mapping, and the Ofsted report. Look at the web site for things that are highlighted, such as grants for particular needs, as this will give you an insight into the school's priorities.

Think about how you could respond if you were asked about the biggest challenge on your last placement. If you answered by just stating that you struggled, for example, with behaviour, this would probably not be favourably received by the interviewing panel. If you stated that you learnt a lot about the importance of setting clear boundaries for children and how things got much better once you and the children discussed and used the class rules, this would demonstrate that you learnt and moved on from your initial challenge. You could also expand by explaining that as you met the learning needs of the children and understood how to engage the children, learning became the primary focus and not behaviour.

You may be asked a question about something that you may not have experienced. For example, you may be asked a question about how you might deal with a parent/carer who is angry. You might reply by saying that you could ask if your mentor could sit in the meeting with you, or if the parent/carer is really angry you could always say you can meet tomorrow after school, giving you time to get some advice. You could state that if you feel you could deal with the situation you would ask the parent to sit down with you, let the parent/carer talk without interrupting so that you can hear what they have to say. You would try to resolve the situation and use inclusive language such as 'working on a solution together' and 'meeting together' soon to see how things are going. At the end of the meeting you could say something along the lines that you are pleased they shared their concerns with you. You would aim to finish the meeting by shaking hands. You could also state that if at any time you felt that you were out of your depth, you would speak to the headteacher or deputy and arrange a meeting. Answering in this way demonstrates that you are able to think through a situation by yourself even though you may not have had any experience.

No school will be expecting a trainee teacher to have the fullest answers to all the questions. What they are looking for is someone who will be open to learning. So if you are unable to give the fullest answer to a question, do not be afraid to state that you have a lot to learn and would always be willing to seek answers from more experienced staff.

You may well be asked about what you can contribute to the school. I would always caution about promising too much. So do not promise that you will take on lots of after school clubs or get involved in too many activities. I would say that your first priority is to the children in your class, meeting all their needs and ensuring that they all make at least good progress. There is always so much to learn and you will need to prioritise. Do say, though, that you understand the importance of getting involved in the wider life of the school and supporting key events.

What questions might you ask the interview panel?

Often at the end of an interview you are asked if you have any questions you would like to ask the panel. You may have had all your queries explained in which case you can politely say that you think everything you needed to know has been answered. You may like to think about asking:

- about the support for newly qualified teachers, what mentoring programme you might receive. Knowing about the support you will receive when entering the teaching profession is really important;
- the year group you would be teaching if you were offered the job. This may be an important factor in your decision as to whether you accept the job;
- how the mission or value statement is embedded into the life of the school;
- how you will be supported in planning in a single form entry school;
- how the school manages social media, especially with parents/carers.

Sometimes the interview panel ask if you would accept the job if you were offered it. Be honest if you are unsure and ask whether you could have some time to think and will get back to them first thing in the morning. It is important that you feel really confident that this is the job that you want.

Smile and think about your body language.

Key elements to include in an observed lesson

Preparation is key to planning for and being observed with a class or group of children that you have not met before.
You need to know:

- the age range of the children;
- how many children;
- if the school can provide resources required (you need to list these but keep the list short and simple);
- if any of the children have any specific needs;
- if there will be any support staff, if there's a particular child they need to be allocated to and how they are usually deployed;
- the routines and rules in the classroom (e.g. chime bells as a sign for quiet);
- the length of the observation;
- what area of the curriculum to teach;
- previous learning.

If you have not been provided with these details do not be afraid to phone up the school and ask. It would also be useful to ask whether the children will have name badges so that you can immediately start using their names. If you require any resources make sure the school knows about any reasonable requests before the day of the observation and make sure that you receive assurances that the resources will be available. Always have a back-up if you are using ICT.

Before the lesson even begins think about how you are going to start the lesson. The children may be lined up outside the classroom waiting for you to take them in. If this is the case, you must be very specific with your instructions about entering the classroom. Introduce yourself to the children and recap on the key class rules that you will be using in the lesson. This demonstrates that you have set your boundaries and you will be able to demonstrate the use of these rules. Give praise when praise is due and make sure absolutely everyone is listening if a child is speaking. If you want the class to transition from a carpet area to tables, allow a few children to move at a time. It is these little but significant points that can make the difference in an observed lesson.

Lesson observation

Useful elements to include in an observed lesson are:

- introducing a visual reminder of the learning question;
- some clear modelling from you;
- planned questions;
- active learning opportunities for the children;
- a mini plenary to refocus learning;
- a plenary to focus on learning (by re-visiting the learning question), any misconceptions and further challenges.

You can finish the lesson by giving the children a challenge whereby you are demonstrating that you can 'hook' them into the next stage of learning. This is a challenge that could be undertaken at home with parents/carers.

Story reading observation

If you are being asked to read a story you will need to plan for:

- class participation;
- key questioning to check understanding as you go;
- predictions.

Choosing a book is so important in terms of being age appropriate and suitable for the amount of time available. You can choose a specific section of a book. The first thing you must do is ensure that all the children can see the book, especially if you are showing the pictures. If this is the case, make sure you scan the book starting with the furthest child to your left, across to the furthest child on your right. Make sure you practise the voices of different characters in the book and do not be afraid or shy to really demonstrate how engaging you can be. Think of the volume of your voice when reading, making sure that you can be really quiet (whilst still making sure all the children can hear) and alter the volume and pace according to the text. Try to raise your head and make eye contact with the children as much as possible.

Your questioning will be really important to demonstrate the children's understanding, so think about this when choosing a book. Using partner talk can be really useful as a way of getting the children talking about the text. If you include partner talk make sure you join in with the discussions. If the lesson does not go as planned do not be afraid to adapt the lesson. You are likely to be asked about the lesson in the interview so you can explain why you deviated from your plan or you could explain what you might do differently on reflection. As well as concentrating on the teaching and learning opportunities in the lesson, you must really demonstrate that you can connect with the children and get them engaged in the lesson.

> *Demonstrate that you can connect with the children you are teaching.*

On most occasions the interview and the observed lesson will be on the same day. Arrive at the school about 10 minutes before the time you are due to arrive. You then have time to freshen up before being called for interview. Do not be tempted to arrive any earlier as the school needs time to prepare for the day ahead.

If you do not get the job you must phone up for feedback. This is the only way you can truly learn from the experience. If you do get the job, it is always worthwhile sending an email to the school thanking them and arranging for a date to come into school for a further chat.

Your digital footprint

You will be preparing for an interview and the school will also be preparing to interview you.

Before sending off your letter of application use a search engine to check what can find be found out about you online, as it is possible that someone on the interview panel will be doing the same thing.

Always make sure that you:

- make social media accounts private;
- use a different name;
- use an appropriate head shot.

It is also wise to get into the habit of regularly checking privacy settings of social media sites as these can be updated. It is also advisable to talk to friends about the importance of your online presence so that they can be aware of what they are positing online about you. There are settings that can make sure you approve of tags or are notified when anyone tags you but it is worthwhile having conversations about the importance of what is posted online at this stage. You may even be asked a question about the personal use of social media and the professional use of social media in the interview.

Finding out whether you have got the job

You will most probably be told by the headteacher whether you have been successful in getting the job so make sure you plan for how you will respond when the call comes through. If you have been successful you need to thank the headteacher and say how much you are looking forward to working in their school. Have pen and paper handy so that you can write down any key information that you may be given.

If you have been unsuccessful, thank the headteacher for the experience and ask if they could possibly give you any specific feedback regarding the interview process. You may have come a very close second to the successful candidate, and if this is the case, it is really good to know that you did well. You can always finish the conversation by stating that if any more jobs become available at the school you would still love to apply. Do not forget that headteachers have a network of contacts and may know of other jobs in the local area.

If you are successful at interview, it is quite hard when you receive that initial phone call to be focused enough to start organising when you should come into the school for your next visit so a follow up email is a good way of doing this. Ensure the email is formally written. Here is an example of the formal nature of the email required:

Dear Mrs. Jones, I would just like to thank you and the interview panel for appointing me to the Year 5 post starting in September. I am really looking forward to working in your school.

Please could I arrange to come in for a meeting with the Year 5 year leader so that I can start getting organised? You also mentioned in the interview that the deputy headteacher, Mr. Humphreys, will be my mentor. Is there any chance I could also meet with him as

I know you wanted me to arrange with him the possibility of attending a Safeguarding course for NQTs in the borough?
I look forward to hearing from you and visiting the school again soon.
Kind regards, Jake Gulbenkian

Summary

Some of the best teachers I know are not the best at being interviewed. This can be really frustrating and perhaps some of the systems for interviewing are better than others. Being as prepared as you possibly can be really helps.

If you are someone who gets really nervous you must be mindful of your body language; make sure you put any bags on the floor and place your hands comfortably in your lap. Practise answering questions with a friend as they will hopefully be honest with you about the little traits you have when nervous, such as wringing your hands or turning a ring around and around on a finger. If you present as confident (even though you may not be feeling confident), the panel should feel confident in you. Remember that the interviewing panel will understand that you are new to the profession and will not have the fullest answers for everything. What they will be interested in is someone who: can connect with children, understands the key ingredients of teaching and learning, is a team player, and is always willing to learn.

Check list

I have:	Tick
◦ collected evidence in a portfolio from my last placement;	
◦ written the main body of a letter of application;	
◦ read the school's values, vision, or mission statement;	
◦ looked in detail at the school's web site;	
◦ searched my name (and nicknames) on the internet to ensure my social media sites are on a 'private' setting.	

CHAPTER 2

Getting ready for the final placement

This chapter should help you to:

- get into the right mind set;
- develop resilience through:
  - being mindful of your well-being
  - considering your role as a mentee
  - using reflection
  - pacing yourself;
- manage your online presence;
- be mindful how you communicate with teachers.

Introduction

This chapter should make you stop and reflect on how you can help yourself plan for the final school placement before even stepping into the school. A final school placement is challenging and you will therefore need to plan for how you are going to look after yourself and to give yourself the best chance of completing a successful placement in preparation for a career in teaching.

Getting into the right mind set

Each placement in a school is a new beginning. It is never helpful to start any new experience highlighting that:

- the teachers on your previous placement thought that you were outstanding;
- you are just 'getting the qualification' as you previously worked in a school (therefore presenting as though you possess all the skills and knowledge already);
- you have a First Class Honours Degree in English, so teaching reading to Year 1 children should not be a problem at all.

An outstanding trainee teacher is someone who is able to be outstanding in different schools, with children of different ages, abilities and needs within the primary phase; this is no mean feat! I have often thought that in the long term, part of the make-up of truly 'great teachers' are those who understand that there is always so much to learn and place their focus on the progress and well-being of the children.

It is useful for a final placement school to know about your background so that mentors can draw on your strengths as well as being prepared to help with your key targets. A very short C.V. is a useful way of presenting this information in a factual way.

Useful information to present to a school:

- first degree (French degree);
- previous jobs (Taught in an international Summer School in France);
- previous experiences of working with children (TA in Year 1 for 3 years);
- hobbies (Play football for a local team);
- key personal information that you are happy to share (I drop my 5-year-old child at the minders at 7:40 and catch the 7:50 bus to school, so should arrive no later than 8:00);
- learning difficulties, disabilities, and medical situations that may require some adjustments.

Receiving information on key strengths and targets would give mentors understanding of your needs and would demonstrate that you are proactive and actively thinking about your own personal development.

Key strengths from previous placement	Evidence	Potential for developing further on final placement
1.		
2.		

Key targets from previous placement	What you have done to prepare for the final placement	Create a related target for the final placement
1.		
2.		

For some trainee teachers, any previous school placements may have been a real challenge. For a small minority, teaching is too much of a challenge and hopefully through self-reflection and discussions with mentors this can be realised. There are many, however, who struggle on their initial placements and then go on to be very successful teachers. Indeed, I have known some who have failed a final placement and then passed the retake with flying colours. There is so much to learn and you never stop learning throughout your career so try to prioritise the key aspects of your practice you need to improve and think about how you might deepen your skills, knowledge, and understanding of these aspects of practice before your final placement. Trainee teachers might think that 'reflection' and 'target setting' is tedious, but if this is done well and becomes part of your practice throughout your career, you will remain open, honest, and deepen your knowledge of pedagogy, thus enabling you to become a more effective teacher. After 18 years of teaching I was still giving myself 1 clear target a term for improvement. These add up over the years! No matter how well you achieved in previous placements every trainee teacher should be acting on key targets set from previous placements. Be proactive. Do not wait for others to organise this for you. I would be really impressed if I was interviewing a candidate for a teaching post and they were not only able to articulate a personal target for their teaching but were able to demonstrate what they had done to start working on the target.

> *Reset yourself. A new placement is a clean sheet, a new beginning, the start of having to demonstrate what you are capable of.*

Resilience and well-being

Resilience is the ability to recover quickly from difficulties. In teaching there will always be challenges that come your way, some expected and some unexpected, such as your observed lesson not going to plan or the ICT equipment failing in the middle of a lesson. These sorts of things happen to absolutely everyone who teaches. When things go wrong try not to dwell on them for too long. We must learn from our mistakes and challenges and also learn to keep things in perspective.

Resilience is also about being flexible, to be able to adapt to changes. This can be quite hard at times when you have spent forever planning a lesson that you have to completely alter because the children are losing concentration or not understanding what is being taught. Have the strength to be confident in being flexible when teaching. If you are being observed you can always explain why you had to make any changes to the lesson plan.

Be aware of what helps you in difficult times. What are the trigger signs that mean you are beginning to feel a bit wobbly and what strategies help you to cope?

You are far more likely to be resilient if you are well prepared for all the expectations of the final placement and plan for your well-being. You will need to give yourself time for intense planning and preparation every day but then still leave time for watching some TV, taking the dog for a walk, speaking to family/friends. Developing positive professional relationships within the community of school is also so important to your well-being. Positive relationships will help when you need to draw on the skills and understanding of others when challenges arise. Resilience and well-being are undoubtedly interlinked.

The following timetable is an example of how you can plan for your well-being as part of everyday life. Adapt this timetable to work for you, but try not to lose the elements of:

1. connecting with others (staff and children);
2. learning from others;
3. being active;
4. helping others;
5. looking after yourself.

Suggested daily routine to incorporate well-being

8:00	■ Arrive at school (try to walk part of the way if possible). ■ Connect with people around the school ensuring a positive *"Good morning."* ■ Start the morning calmly with the children and get into a routine. ■ Drink water throughout the morning. It is easy to forget.
12:00–13:00	■ 20 minutes 'setting up' for the afternoon. ■ 15 minutes brisk walk. ■ 15 minutes having lunch in the staff room. ■ 10 minutes back in the classroom quietly thinking about the afternoon session.
13:15–15.30	■ Start the afternoon calmly with the children and get into a routine. ■ Drink water throughout the afternoon. ■ Finish the day positively with the children: *"Today we have learnt to. . . . I am proud of you!"* ■ Give some positive feedback to parents/carers. ■ Thank people who have helped you today.

15.30–16:00	■ Have a cup of tea and talk to other staff. ■ Talk about things that went well and also your challenges. ■ Let others know that you are learning from them: "*I loved the learning wall in your classroom.*" ■ Just sit and be quiet sometimes or give to others. "*I've got 15 minutes so can I help you with that display?*"
16:00–18:00	■ Planning/marking/preparation time. ■ Get as much done as you can in this 2-hour slot. ■ Set up the classroom for the next day: books on desk, challenge on the interactive whiteboard, etc. (this should help you to stop thinking about all the things you have to get ready in the morning).
18:00–20:00	■ Get home . . . try to walk part of the way. ■ Make these 2 hours your own. ■ Cook a healthy meal.
20:00–21:00	■ Final preparation for tomorrow. ■ Completing any paper work, etc. so that you feel as prepared as possible.
21:00	■ Make this your time before bed. ■ Go to bed early. ■ Switch off all electronic devices.

- After school on a Friday night be aware of planning and resources required for the next week that will help you with planning over the weekend. Stay until 6 o'clock to ensure marking, etc. is completed.
- Friday night should be a night off!
- Try to have 1 full day at the weekend when you are not doing school work.

Remember, if you look after your well-being, you are far more likely to be resilient.

Resilience and being a mentee

Much is written about the skills of being a mentor but less is written about the skills of being a mentee and the responsibilities that this role entails. Before you start your final placement think about your attitude to being mentored. Your mentor certainly has a responsibility towards you and your development as a trainee teacher but you also need to be aware of your role and responsibilities. You need to take ownership and be proactive in developing a positive relationship with your mentor. Taking ownership and being proactive should help you to develop your resilience. Here are some things that you can actively prepare for and think about before the official start of the placement.

Organise a time to meet every week

I have heard many times from trainee teachers that their mentor is so busy and that it is hard to find a time to meet. Indeed, the people who are given the role of mentor are often in senior leadership positions and have many responsibilities. So before the final placement even begins, perhaps on your initial visit to the school and in a meeting with your mentor, try to organise a set meeting time every week throughout the final placement. This meeting does not need to be longer than 30 minutes. You must acknowledge that there may be occasions when you will have to be adaptable and meet your mentor at a different time to the time that was planned.

Weekly meeting

In the weekly meeting ensure that you take notes. Many mentors have stated that, when this happens they feel as though the mentee is listening attentively and taking on board the advice. Also this may be a time for the mentee to clarify any points/targets made. Write down your targets for the following week and try to articulate to your mentor how you might try to address the targets.

Use the following questions to self-reflect on your role as a mentee

How open are you to receiving constructive feedback?	■ Visualise your body language when you are given feedback; ■ seek clarification of feedback if required but take on board constructive feedback; ■ thank your mentor.
How well do you actively work on your targets?	If a target is to include more open questions demonstrate to your mentor how: ■ you have included key questioning in your planning; ■ you have asked your class teacher to observe and give you feedback on your questioning in the introduction of a lesson; ■ you would like your mentor to give you feedback on your questioning at the next observation.
Do you hear the positive feedback?	■ Write down the positive things your mentor says and look at them every day; ■ thank your mentor (acknowledging that you have heard the positive).
Summarise the key points of the meeting and write them down.	■ At the end of the meeting briefly summarise the key points as this should help clarification.

Comparing mentors' expectations!

Throughout my time with working with trainee teachers, one of their bugbears has been the fact that they believe mentors have different expectations. I therefore pose this question to you: would you as a teacher have different expectation from the children in your class? Of course you would, because they are all individuals with different needs and different abilities—whilst of course you have high expectations for all. When you have a one to one observation and feedback and discussion with your mentor, this scenario provides an ideal opportunity for personalised learning, providing targets and expectations to meet the individual needs of the trainee. Therefore please try not to compare yourself with other trainee teachers. You may be expected to plan for an intervention group in week 3 of the final placement because your mentor thinks you are capable. Remember that every school setting and every class of children is different so it is impossible to compare experiences.

Concentrate on your development and journey as a trainee teacher.

Resilience and reflection

Your weekly meetings with your mentor are really important and it is crucial to be honest with them about how you are feeling. *"This week has been a real struggle, but I think I am beginning to understand how to implement assessment for learning into my lessons more successfully."* Demonstrate how you have persevered in trying to meet a key target.

The process of writing a weekly reflection based on your targets should allow you to take time out and really analyse your practice and to ascertain whether you have made progress. Take yourself somewhere quiet and reflect honestly. Do not just retell what has happened but analyse how you have made alterations to your practice. Recognising small but significant changes is important. Share these with your mentor to demonstrate how you are really taking on board all the advice they are giving you.

I have seen some excellent reflections that have been a real testament to trainee teachers who have demonstrated a high level of perseverance in tackling an element of their practice that initially seemed an insurmountable problem. Reflections can also be used to analyse when things go really well, celebrating successes and demonstrating that trainee teachers have the strength and ability to move on from earlier challenges.

Resilience and pacing yourself

In advance, plan for the 'pinch points' of the final placement. When are you likely to be most tired? Do you have key assessment points? When are your observations?

When are your mentor meetings? Plan for these key points throughout the final placement by undertaking your own 'Pacing Myself' mapping exercise. A couple of aspects of pacing yourself are focusing on your key targets, rather than trying to improve on too many aspects of your practice at once, and being organised.

Pacing yourself is also about keeping paper work up to date at all times. On a final placement it is almost impossible to try to 'catch up' on paper work half way through as you will be teaching for a significant amount of time. The paper work should be integral to the placement, demonstrating understanding of practice. It is also a way of showing that you are able to meet deadlines and adhere to expectations.

Example of 'Pacing Myself'

Week 1
- Collect all key information to present in a well ordered file ready to present at your first observation in week 2.
- Get in the habit of being organised and up to date with all requirements.
- Do not be tempted to teach too much too soon.
- Do not be tempted to volunteer for a club too soon.

Week 2 (first formal observation)
- Plan for this observation at least 2 days before so that you can seek help if required.
- Ensure all resources are sourced and in place the day before.

Week 3
- The teaching load is likely to be increased this week. If you are teaching all morning ensure all resources are ready before the start of the school day.
- Ensure you spend time with your TA. If you fully engage them in terms of planning and preparation and deploy them effectively, they will be able to help.
- Be systematic in collecting evidence of: how you are addressing targets from observation 1; pupil progress (in a lesson or series of lessons).

Week 4 (second formal observation and mid-point review of your progress)
- Try to keep the weekend before as free as possible in preparation for this week.
- Ensure that targets from observation 1 are clearly addressed in planning and delivery of the observed lesson.
- At this point resilience is required as you will be tired. Always remember: targets are not a criticism.

Half Term
- Re-charge!
- Be positive in being proactive with the targets given at the mid-point review.
- Meet with a tutor from your training institution for additional advice if necessary.

Week 5
- Observe excellent practice in your school in relation to your key targets.
- Be proactive in implementing what you have learnt from these observations.

Week 6 (formal observation 3)
- Ensure that targets from observation 2 are clearly addressed in planning and delivery of the observed lesson.
- Use your mentor meeting to ensure that you have a clear expectation of what you need to achieve by the end of the placement.

Week 7
Spend weeks 7, 8, and 9 focusing on key targets.
- Ask a teacher to watch you for 10 minutes and give you feedback.
- Do not be too hard on yourself if 1 lesson in a week is awful—this happens to everyone! Focus on all the lessons that went well. Learn from your mistakes and move on.

Week 8
- Focus on your own development as a teacher.
- Observe excellent practice of a subject that you find more of a challenge. Team teach this subject if necessary.

Week 9 (formal observation 4)
- Ensure your file of evidence is up to date for your mentor. If you have paced yourself and kept up to date with the paper work you should not find this time consuming. The paper work should be integral to your practice and not an 'add on'.

Week 10 (final assessment conference of your progress)
- You should contribute to your final conference. Ensure you present evidence to demonstrate your progress.

Managing your online presence

Chapter 1 on applying for a job and an interview gives advice about checking your online presence by putting your name and possible nicknames into a search engine in order to check what can be accessed about you online. Make sure you do this before the start of your final placement and that your social media accounts:

- are private;
- use a different name;
- use an appropriate head shot.

Also make sure that you regularly check the privacy settings of the social media sites you use as these often change. Remind your friends that you are on final placement in a school setting and they must be mindful of any posts they make that include you.

Use settings that can make sure you approve of tags or are notified when anyone tags you.

The best policy is to be careful about what you post online so that you protect your professional reputation. Remember whatever is posted will always be there.

Be aware of the school's guidelines on the use of the internet and technology. Always:

- act according to the school's policy;
- use the school's computers as they should have appropriate filters;
- apply 'safety modes' (Google—safe search, YouTube—safety mode);
- use the school's cameras and other electronic devices and know the school's policy on how any data is stored;
- search a web site immediately prior to teaching as content on the internet changes so quickly; make sure you have done your homework and know exactly what content will be seen by the children. You cannot rely on something that you researched and viewed last term.

It is imperative that as a trainee teacher you are aware of up to date information. You must therefore be proactive in ensuring that you are fully knowledgeable and understand all current legislation and advice. At the time of writing this, 'Childnet' (https://childnet.com/teachers-and-professionals) has really superb and accessible resources, with guides for teachers such as:

- professional reputation;
- using technology;
- Social Media Guide for Teachers and Support Staff;
- Teachers Technology Checklist.

Spend a few hours searching for and reading advice before starting your final placement. Also be aware of current Department for Education statutory documents on keeping children safe in education.

Communicating with teachers

Texting

Texting can be useful but always be aware that texts can be misinterpreted and have the capacity to look unprofessional. I would advise against using emojis as not everyone understands their meaning and they can be misunderstood. It is very easy to slip into a more casual mode of communication with some colleagues. I would advise against this and remember you are a mentee.

Emails

Books have been written about the mistakes that have been made when words have been spelt incorrectly and caused offence because the meaning of the email has been altered. Whenever you are writing to colleagues ensure every email is written professionally. I always write emails with the understanding that any can be recalled and seen by any of my work colleagues. This really helps me think about what I write. Also do not write emails or anything of importance when you are in a rush as mistakes are likely to be made. In addition, confidential or sensitive information should never be communicated in an email and names should never be used.

Phones in school

You must not have your phone on in any lesson. Any use of phones must be away from children. Schools may have policies on the use of phones in staff spaces so do check.

Never name the school or people working at the school in any writing, even on your private social media sites.

Summary

Being prepared is key to being successful on this final placement. I have seen many trainee teachers who have coasted in the first phase of their final placement and then found it really hard to catch up and produce credible evidence that will help them pass. There is so much to do and so much to learn, so being really systematic in your approach to what is required should really help you. Part of being a great teacher is demonstrating that you can cope with the pressure points and meet deadlines and so being organised will help you to demonstrate that you can meet these expectations. Also an important part of this process is managing to look after yourself. Plan for your well-being just as you plan systematically for the final placement; this in turn should help your resilience.

Check list

	Tick
I have:	
◦ created a simple C.V. for my mentor and class teacher that will help them understand my strengths and areas for development;	
◦ thought about how I can build in daily routines that will help my well-being;	
◦ checked my social media sites are set to 'private'.	
I can name 2 things that I can develop on this placement that will help me be a better mentee;	
I know the 'pinch points' in my final placement.	

CHAPTER 3

Managing relationships

This chapter should help you to:

- be mindful of the importance of first impressions;
- develop positive relationships with:
  - your mentor
  - your class teacher;
- understand the deployment of other staff in the classroom;
- develop your understanding of communicating with parents and carers;
- understand the importance of being part of the community of school.

Introduction

Teaching can be considered a science, an art, or a craft but it is also about having the ability to form professional working relationships with people within the school environment as well as the community of parents and carers. This chapter should help you to think about how you can plan for opportunities that could help you to develop this aspect of your practice.

First impressions

Meeting your mentor for the first time

When you go into school for the first time you should be going in with confidence that you are aware of all the expectations required for the placement. You should have read all documentation really thoroughly. Do remember that whilst your school experience is absolutely everything to you, for your mentor the role is just one of their many different responsibilities. At the first meeting think about what might be the most pertinent pieces of information that you need to highlight. An example of a short list of documentation/information might be:

■ key documentation
  ○ Safeguarding policy and information about the role of the designated safeguarding lead;
  ○ Staff Behaviour policy (sometimes called the code of conduct or Staff Handbook)
	This must include evidence of knowing the name of the safeguarding lead in the school (this is essential information to have on a first meeting).

■ the weekly expectations in terms of teaching and preparation time;	*This will help the mentor to build up the expectations gradually. Be aware that these expectations are usually adapted by each school.*
■ the number and pattern of formal observations required in the placement;	*It is useful for your mentor to plan these in advance (at this stage it is usually just plotting the week of the observation).*
■ the documentation for the weekly meeting with your mentor (e.g. key targets, reflections etc.);	*Having the formal documentation required for the weekly meeting will alert your mentor to the requirements of your training institution.*
■ targets from previous placement as well as key successes.	*This will help your mentor to personalise your experience and to focus on key aspects of your practice.*

You will bring with you all the wealth of experience from previous work/life experiences. Think of presenting these in a format as laid out in Chapter 2 ('Useful information to present to a school'). This will possibly give your mentor an idea of what responsibilities or teaching experiences to give you. For example, if you have a French degree your mentor may give you a French group to teach early on in the placement.

In this first meeting, it may also be useful to ask when your non-contact time is timetabled. It is much more useful to get this sorted out early on so that you can get into a routine for planning and preparation. Think about how you might ask for this information: "*I want to be as thoroughly prepared as possible, so is there any chance of knowing when my non-contact time could be?*"

Present yourself as organised in this meeting. Make notes on what your mentor is telling you.

> *Try to present as open, friendly, organised, and professional.*

Developing a positive relationship with your mentor

Building a positive relationship with your mentor is partly about demonstrating that you are actively trying to meet the targets that are being set at the weekly meeting. In Chapter 2 you hopefully self-reflected on your role as a mentee. Now you need to put all your self-reflection into practice. You need to prepare for these meetings with evidence of how you have been trying to meet targets. For example, if your target was to include more assessment for learning (AfL) opportunities in lessons you can demonstrate this:

- in planning;
- by asking your class teacher to observe you teach an introduction to a lesson that uses key AfL questions and ask for brief feedback which can be used in the mentor meeting;
- in a reflection written by you analysing the outcomes of including AfL in teaching and learning opportunities.

If a mentee is prepared for a meeting in this way it really demonstrates that they are taking on board advice and acting on it. Be prepared to be open and honest about things that have gone well and things that have been a struggle. These meetings should be a dialogue with specific outcomes but in order to achieve this, you need to have an active voice that contributes to the conversation. Equally you need to be a good listener and take on board advice given. If you are really struggling with an aspect of your practice, ask if it is possible to have some specific help.

Specific help	Guidance
Film or tape yourself teaching	If you agree to be filmed or taped and have permission, this could be used in a mentor meeting as a tool for analysing practice. Alternatively, you could look at or listen to a recording by yourself and analyse your practice.
	Always delete films and tapes and listen/watch in school. Get advice from the person in charge of data protection in school.
Focused observation	You can be observed with a specific focus on one of your targets (e.g. AfL). Ensure the target is evidenced in your planning.
Shared observation with your mentor	You could watch a section of a qualified teacher's lesson with your mentor with a particular focus, e.g. AfL.

There are many teachers in a school that could help you to develop certain aspects of your practice. The school is a community of practitioners and as a trainee teacher you are in a unique position to be able to observe the best practice possible across the school.

In weekly meetings with your mentor aim to:

- demonstrate how you have addressed the previous week's targets;
- explain what has gone particularly well and what you feel you need to work on next;
- demonstrate evidence of pupil progress and evidence of things that you are proud of;
- write down the key points from the meeting.

These points should be encompassed within the dialogue in the meeting, but demonstrating that you are taking ownership and being proactive in your practice should help to develop a professional working relationship with your mentor. Being prepared and having everything up to date demonstrates a professional approach.

First impressions

The first week with your class teacher

This is the person who you are going to be working with on a daily basis throughout the placement. You will be entering their classroom with their routines, class rules, and hidden rules already established. I have often told trainee teachers that working alongside a teacher on final placement is like cooking in someone else's kitchen: you have to fit in and find out the ways in which things are done, as well as develop your own style of teaching.

It is useful to explain to your teacher that having time for some focused observations on aspects of teaching and learning would be really useful. After observing briefly, tell the teacher what you have learnt. Sometimes teachers want you to get involved in teaching straight away, so explaining how useful observations can be demonstrates that you are learning. Be mindful to have a balance throughout those first few days of observing as well as getting involved with teaching and learning. In this way, you will start to build your confidence with the children and start to develop your teacher presence in the class.

Things that will get you off to a positive start:

- ensure you arrive in good time and leave when everything is organised for the next day;
- offer to help with marking (this first week would be an excellent time to co-mark with your class teacher);
- get involved with playground duties;
- have a story, song, or activity that you have chosen and offer to take the class at the end of the day.

Things you need to know in the first week:

- your teaching commitment for the following week;
- an overview of the topics to be taught in the placement so that you can develop/deepen your subject or pedagogic knowledge if necessary;
- any specific needs (including medical) of the children in your class;
- class data;
- school behaviour policy and how this translates into the classroom practice and routines.

The first week is about setting the firm foundations for the weeks ahead. You will have so many questions but remember that you will not find out everything you want to know straight away. Think about the key pieces of information you need. Your class teacher will be able to give you some time but be mindful of the teacher's other responsibilities.

Pace yourself.

Start with finding out the key information you need to know.

Developing a positive relationship with your class teacher

Your class teacher should inform your mentor of the progress you are making and whilst they may not be undertaking formal observations of you teaching, they will be giving you informal feedback on a daily basis. They may well be involved in interim assessments as well as your final report. If possible, jot down what they tell you so that they can see that you are taking on board their advice. Also, after the weekly meeting with your mentor make sure you share your targets and reflections with your class teacher.

You could ask your class teacher to help you with some specific help.

Specific help	Guidance
Focused observation	Ask your teacher to observe you for 10 minutes and give you feedback on an aspect of your practice, e.g. differentiated questions.
Team teaching	Maybe teaching gymnastics is a real worry for you, so ask your teacher if you can plan together and team teach. Over time you can increase your teaching time as your confidence grows.

Specific help	Guidance
Coaching	The mentor can quietly give advice or give agreed signals to you during a lesson.

Asking your class teacher to get involved has the potential to develop the working relationship and demonstrates that you value their input. Once the children in the class have got used to you teaching them and you have demonstrated to your class teacher that you have used their strategies to good effect, you should be able to start to develop your own ideas. This has to be undertaken with great tact, especially when planning is established. The language of possibilities should be used. For example,

"If I keep the same learning objective, is there any chance I could try out some different learning activities?"

"Is there any possibility of me trying to introduce an emotions chart when taking the register?"

At year group planning meetings, make sure that you start to bring ideas to the table and begin to gently offer to undertake one of the weekly plans. It is this awareness and sensitivity of working as part of the team that will help embed you into the collegiate working atmosphere of a school. When you are responsible for planning, always make sure it is available to everyone in good time prior to teaching.

Things to consider

Occasionally working with your class teacher may be a challenge but this is the world of work and the professional working relationships we all have to develop. If this is the case, you will have to be proactive in building up the relationship. Thank them for feedback and tell them that you will focus on a certain aspect of your practice the next day. Do always greet everyone with a positive "*Good morning*" and after school ask if there is anything you can help them with. Offer to make a cup of tea.

It is sometimes easy to build up a great friendship with your class teacher during the placement and you can end up texting them as if they are your best friend. I would always be mindful of the fact that, for the duration of the placement, you need to have a professional relationship. Informal texts and social encounters can be misinterpreted and send mixed messages, so it is best to always remember you are being assessed.

The deployment of other staff in the classroom

Teaching assistants (TAs) or learning support assistants (LSAs) will have established working relationships with the class teacher. Initially you therefore need to mirror what is already happening in the classroom in terms of planning, preparation, and the deployment of additional adults. It can be quite daunting for TAs and LSAs to suddenly start working with someone new in the middle of an academic year and to understand the dynamics of working with a trainee teacher. It can also be daunting for you as the additional adults may well have vast experiences of working with children and know individual children's needs. But this is something that you must harness; acknowledge their skills and understanding of the children whilst also developing your understanding of leading the planning and teaching opportunities. Drawing on the skills of others who are already working with the children is key to building up positive relationships.

Some ways of finding out about the additional adults you will be working with is to:

- get to know their roles (TA/LSA);
- find out which subjects they really like;
- let them know in advance what is happening in lessons and their involvement;
- ask for their feedback on the progress of the children they have been supporting;
- ensure you involve the additional adults and the children they have been supporting in key phases of the lesson;
- thank them at the end of the lesson and in front of the class use inclusive language e.g. "*Mr. Johansson and I really enjoyed that lesson and think you all tried really hard.*"

As the placement progresses, you should be able to develop some of your own ideas, such as assessment sheets that the TA can briefly fill in for you at the end of a teaching session, so that you are aware of the progress of the children and can plan accordingly for the next session. Go gently with new ideas and reflect with the TA/LSA on the effectiveness of any new method of collecting information. Thank them for trying out your idea.

Remember that with any additional adults in the classroom, you should be planning for and leading the learning opportunities for the children and not expecting the additional adults to differentiate for you. Even though you are developing your role as the 'lead' in the classroom, using the language of possibilities is useful:

"*Mrs. Singh, could you possibly try leading the focus group using this computer program? Can you let me know what you think about it? Thanks!*"

"Mr. Davies, could we try to use blue ink on a white background for Sam's writing? Let's see if it helps."

It is often these little nuances in professional interactions that make a difference to someone wanting to work for you as opposed to having to work for you.

Relationships build up gradually through mutual trust and respect.

Developing understanding of communicating with parents/carers

Learning how to build up relationships with parents/carers on a final placement is not always easy but take every opportunity to meet with parents/carers by:

- meeting and greeting in the morning;
- talking to a parent/carer at the end of the school day, especially about something positive a child has achieved;
- asking parents/carers to come in for the last 5 minutes of school to look at something the class have achieved;
- setting homework/getting involved in reading diaries;
- asking if you can sit in on a few parent/carer consultations;
- asking if you can sit in on a SENCO/Inclusion manager meeting with a parent/carer.

Being part of the community of school

As well as being a teacher in your classroom, you are learning to be a professional in a community of teachers in school. You therefore need to demonstrate that you can form professional working relationships with all people within the school.
This will be helped by:

- simple everyday courtesies to everyone in the school environment;
- eating your lunch in the staff room—this can be a little daunting at first but it is key to building up relationships;
- giving planning to others in good time;
- getting involved in whole school events such as a Christmas Fayre;
- being wary of staff social events—people let their guards down and this can become tricky;
- helping others, e.g. help to put up a display.

Sometimes you also have to develop an understanding that there may be times when the staff are under pressure or feeling particularly tired. You need to be sensitive to these times and understand that others around you also have pressures.

Summary

Understanding the importance of developing positive relationships cannot be underestimated in a school environment and there are very many different types of professional relationships you need to develop. If nurtured, these relationships can help to provide a secure support framework which can potentially help develop your practice as a trainee teacher. You will need to play a part in gradually building up these relationships and understand that this might take a little time and care. Being seen as a team member in a school is important, demonstrating that you are willing to give as well as receive help.

Check list

	Tick
I am:	
◦ prepared for meetings with my mentor;	
◦ able to ask for specific help from my mentor/class teacher.	
I have shared planning with TAs/LSAs;	
I can demonstrate how I can work as a member of a team;	
I spend some time in the staff room socialising;	
I attend staff meetings and contribute when appropriate.	

CHAPTER 4

Thorough preparation

This chapter should help you to:

- be mindful of and act within the key policies of:
  - safeguarding
  - behaviour
  - marking;
- be prepared for sound subject knowledge and pedagogical knowledge;
- understand class data:
  - progress data
  - special needs
  - English as an additional language.

Introduction

There are many things that you have to consider on your final placement but there are key aspects of your practice that you need to be aware of and address as soon as possible.

This chapter will address key school policies that you will need to understand and adhere to as well as key data that should have the potential to impact on planning for teaching and learning. The progress of all the children in your final placement class must be a key focus of this final placement.

Safeguarding

As a trainee teacher you must take time before a placement in any school begins to make sure you have read all the current and key documentation for safeguarding and child protection and to refresh your understanding of what you have learnt from your training institution.

Everyone is responsible for safeguarding. You therefore have a responsibility to:

- ensure that you engage with all the relevant and up to date documentation from the Department for Education and highlight the sections that you think may be pertinent to you on your placement and keep copies of this key documentation in your file;
- read the school's Safeguarding and Child Protection Policies;
- know the name of the Designated Safeguarding Lead (DSL) in the school and their role within the school.

In the first meeting with your mentor you should demonstrate that you not only have the key documentation in your file but that you have actively engaged with the documentation.

Your mentor and/or class teacher may impart confidential information to you about children you will teach on your final placement. This information must stay confidential.

When writing weekly reflections or assignments that draw on your experiences in school, no school or child should be able to be identified.

If you ever have any concerns about a child in your care ensure that you follow the school's procedures. This is why it is so important to have an understanding of these procedures right at the beginning of placement.

An aspect of safeguarding that trainee teachers can easily miss is the use of IT programmes and clips from the internet. Check with the safeguarding lead and/or IT lead if there is anything that you should be aware of in terms of alerts that have been given to schools.

Behaviour

Every school should have a behaviour policy. It is important to adhere to this policy from the beginning of placement. Schools may differ in the content of their policies. Some schools have a policy of putting names on the board if a child misbehaves and in other schools putting names on the board is banned. Demonstrating to the children that you know and understand the school and class rules and systems is a key part of demonstrating and developing your 'teacher presence' in the classroom. The children will sense if you are unsure and may feel unsettled if you start the placement by bringing new systems into their learning environment.

Within the first few days of placement, ask your class teacher if you can have some time to discuss the school and class rules with the children. This is an absolutely crucial session as it sets out the behaviour guidelines for the rest of the final placement. The children need to know that you understand the rules and will abide by them.

A good way to start is: *"I'm really looking forward to working with you in the next few weeks. I think I know the school rules but can you remind me?"* Develop the discussion by asking the children the reasons for the rules. It can then be highlighted that rules are crucial for a safe and happy learning environment. This session can help to build up positive relationships and a positive classroom ethos. The idea of a discussion is important as this sets the tone for the placement: you are developing a shared understanding between yourself and the children.

Do the same for class rules. If class rules are not displayed in the classroom, ask the class teacher if this would be possible to do. You should make a point of ensuring you overly use the visual prompt in the classroom in the first few days.

"Are we allowed to shout out? What did you tell me the rule was? Let's have a look. Yes, hands up! Now you have your hand up, Tom, you can answer."

"The class rule is listening when someone is speaking. I'll wait until absolutely everyone is listening to what Rheka has to say."

"Remember the school rule of walking and not running."

Actively using the rules in this way should help you to establish yourself in the classroom and the children should feel more settled. One of the first things I ask trainee teachers who have struggled with behaviour management is whether they have taken the time to discuss the school and class rules with the children and to overly use this knowledge in the first few days (at least) of placement. Invariably the answer is no. Children will push the boundaries if they think you do not know or use the boundaries.

Demonstrate your confidence and knowledge to the children.

Behaviour and learning

Behaviour and learning are linked. Children can become restless if they:

- listen for too long;
- are engaged in limited approaches to learning;
- do not have a chance to answer questions or to ask questions;
- are expected to concentrate on a learning activity for too long;
- are not challenged or cannot access learning;
- do not see the point in learning.

This can be helped by:

- cutting down your input by being precise and using prompts and visuals;
- thinking of different ways in which children learn (drawing, acting, sorting/labelling/recording/computer programs);
- using partner talk or group talk opportunities;
- chunking learning by planning for mini plenaries and teaching opportunities;
- ensuring all children can access the learning and are challenged;
- giving reasons and purposes for learning.

Throughout my career, I have talked about the 'light and shade' of planning for learning. This means that I have always sought to ensure that the children encounter a number of different learning opportunities throughout a day and a week. In other words, they should not be sitting down, writing in near silence for a whole day. There should be quiet times but there should also be active learning with plenty of talking opportunities. Providing a variety of learning opportunities should help with the behaviour of the children.

Transitions

Transitions throughout the day are important in ensuring a calm atmosphere. Initially you must follow the routines of the class teacher. Some examples of helping transition are ensuring that:

- you allow the children some 'wriggle time' when they have been sitting down for a long period of time. For example, after assembly, line up the children outside the classroom and get them to copy a few exercises. Explain your expectations before allowing the children to enter the classroom;
- when moving from the carpet area to tables, allow 1 group of children at a time to move;
- if a child finds it difficult to line up with the rest of the class, make them your 'helper' holding equipment at the front of the line;
- before going into a hall or outside for PE, ensure the children know what to do once they enter the space.

Behaviour and language

The way in which language is used can have an enormous impact on the climate of the learning environment. It is a positive step to try to actively think about the language we use. Getting into the routine of using particular phrases can help, especially when you get tired and are likely to drift into using more negative responses.

Negative responses	Positive responses
"Jack, I am waiting for you again!"	"Well done all those children who have put their pens down and are looking this way."
"Put your comic on my desk."	"You can either put your comic on my desk or in your drawer."
"You are not going to lunch until everything is packed away."	"It's nearly lunchtime so let's make sure we are packed away on time."
"Do not shout out."	"What is the class rule about hands up? Well done, Marika, you have now put your hand up so I will ask you to answer the question."
"We haven't got time for your favourite song today as you are taking far too long to tidy up."	"When you have tidied up, we can sing our favourite song."

Remember that, throughout your career, you will be learning about how to manage different behaviours. You may have a child whose behaviour is particularly challenging. Do not expect to make a difference straight away and ensure you seek advice from others on how to deal with particular behaviours. It may even be necessary to ignore certain behaviours. The most important aspect of being the teacher of a child who presents with more challenging behaviour is to build up a positive relationship with the child, so recognise and praise effort when appropriate and remember every day is a new day.

A calm teacher often has a calm class.

Marking

You need to know the marking policy of the school in the first week of placement. You must make sure that you have the permission of the class teacher before you write in any books.

It would be really positive to co-mark with your class teacher in order to understand how the marking policy is used in practice and to then offer to help with marking.

Remember marking should:

- help inform planning (if children have not understood something this should be picked up in the next lesson);
- alert you to whether children are being challenged.

Subject knowledge and pedagogic knowledge

You must prepare for the subject knowledge that is required for the age range you are teaching on this final placement. So it is important to know what you will be teaching in the weeks ahead so that you can practise. The knowledge of phonics, for example, is crucial in understanding and using the correct articulation of sound. It is also worthwhile early on in the placement observing excellent teaching in any area of the curriculum you might be worried about. You may be very confident in Mathematics but the teaching of long division to Year 6 children may be very different to what you have encountered before, so check up on the methods of teaching as well as the content. If, for example, you are teaching Viking raids in History, you will have brushed up on your knowledge and understanding of this period in British History. You will not know everything so if you are asked a question to which you do not know the answer, get the children to look it up. Creating a classroom ethos of 'teacher as learner' and seeking answers as a class can be positive.

If you observe the youngest and then the oldest children in a primary school, you will notice the different pedagogical approaches used by the teachers. It is therefore wise to observe excellent practice of teachers in the age group you will be teaching on final placement. Notice how different pedagogical approaches:

- motivate and engage different children in learning opportunities;
- capture evidence of progress.

Observe excellent practice in a Year 1 class to see how the children can be motivated to speak, listen, interact, and write through a carefully and jointly constructed role play area.

Observe excellent practice in Year 6 to see how children can be motivated to work in a group that mirrors, for example, roles in journalism, to construct the front page of a school newspaper. Also notice how teachers choose different learning opportunities for children within a lesson so that all may successfully access learning. Potentially you can learn a great deal from observations.

Progress data

On previous placements you may not have focused on all the available data on your class. On this placement it is crucial to develop your understanding of how a class teacher needs to engage with the data. The data collected will depend on the age of the child. Key points in summative assessment data is usually:

- at the end of the Early Years Foundation Stage;
- at the end of Key Stage 1 (Year 2);
- at the end of Key Stage 2 (Year 6).

The details of these end of stage assessments are often changed slightly year on year, so do check on expectations. The end of Key Stage summative data for teacher assessments is usually moderated within the local authority. Also moderation across and within year groups usually occurs in a school. Do try to get involved in any moderation processes.

Find out which systems for the collection of assessment data are used in your final placement school and ask if you can get involved with the collection and inputting of data. Book a time early on in the placement to speak to the assessment lead and ask how data has the potential to impact on termly, weekly, and daily planning. Trainee teachers do not often engage with this information early enough in their final placement but it is crucial to do so as the use of assessment and progress data will be important in your first teaching job. Even though schools may use different systems for the collection and analysis of data, it is important to develop your understanding of not just collecting data but using the data for the planning of future learning opportunities.

Assessment for learning should have the biggest impact on children's progress during your final placement. This will be addressed in the next chapter.

Special needs

You will need to have all the relevant information on those children you teach who have special educational needs and/or disabilities (SEND). Depending on the needs of the individual children you will need to ensure that they can access learning. Remember that a teaching assistant should not be used to differentiate as this is your responsibility.

Things to think about:

- not allowing reading and writing to become a barrier to learning;
- providing visuals, prompts, and scaffolds;
- the use of computer programs;
- ensuring that you plan to teach any children with SEND just as much as the other children in the class;
- if a child has difficulty sitting still for periods of time, they are going to need to move, so plan movement into your lesson.

It is important that you understand the specific needs of each individual child. A child with dyslexia, for example, may have different needs to another child in the class with dyslexia. Find out what helps each individual child learn and then undertake some research of your own to help you develop your practice.

The following charts highlight just a few considerations for children on the autistic spectrum and for those children with speech, language, and communication needs. When you analyse the pedagogical approaches to consider when teaching, they are likely to help all children learn.

Autistic spectrum	Some pedagogical considerations may be:
Social understanding	■ planning carefully for learning opportunities that require paired or group work; ■ thinking about the physical space required for learning;
Social communication	■ being wary of sarcasm, jokes, and literal interpretation; ■ understanding that your facial expressions may be hard to read;
Flexible thinking and social imagination	■ thinking about how you will need to plan for new situations; ■ understanding that engaging in activities that require imagination may be difficult (even though the child may be highly imaginative).

Speech, language, and communication	Some pedagogical considerations may be:
Time for responses	■ allowing time for questions to be answered; ■ giving the child prior warning that you will ask them a certain question;
Be aware of giving too much information at once	■ being aware of how much you talk; ■ chunk information—do not give a list of instructions all at once;
Dealing with spoken language mistakes	■ not correcting a child but modelling the correct version, e.g. if a child says, "*We going to theatre today.*" Say, "*Yes, we are going to the theatre today.*"

Know the needs of individual children and research to deepen your understanding.

English as an additional language

It is evident when some children are in the very early stages of learning the English language but it is often surprising how quickly they are able to develop their use of English in social situations. It is important to understand that there is a difference between being socially proficient in a language and being able to access the language of academic learning.

When you analyse the pedagogical approaches that are likely to help children for whom English is an additional language, it is evident that these approaches have the potential to help all children learn.

Some basics to consider when teaching are:	You must think about:
the use of visuals and key language;	■ using the visuals and key language when you are teaching; ■ using visuals outside the classroom, for example, if you are teaching Drama in the hall;
demonstrating that you value their first language;	■ labelling key visuals in first and second languages; ■ learning a few basic words in the child's first language;
planning for opportunities to learn through talk;	■ choosing 'talk partners' carefully;
modelling and scaffolding learning;	■ ensuring that your modelling is clear; ■ providing opportunities for children to model learning to each other;
being mindful of how much you talk.	■ being precise in your use of language.

Just managing to address these key elements of your practice is challenging if it is done really well.

There is so much to learn at this stage so concentrate on key elements of your practice.

Summary

The more you study about teaching and learning and the more time you spend in school, the more you begin to realise just how much there is to learn and this can seem daunting and a little overwhelming at times. If you start by concentrating on the key elements, outlined in this chapter, you should be setting firm foundations on which to develop your understanding of the implementation of key policies as well as developing your pedagogical understanding. Being as prepared as you can should help you to be successful in your final placement. It may feel a little like juggling balls: you feel as though you are coping really well and then you take your eye off a certain aspect of your practice and things begin to slip a little. For example, you may have felt in the first few weeks that the behaviour of the class had improved significantly. However, after a half term holiday the children may seem to have forgotten one of the basic class rules such as putting their hand up to answer a question. If this is the case, go back to basics and return to the class rules, using them pointedly in lessons. Take ownership and actively seek out excellent practitioners to help you develop certain aspects of your practice. Every now and again, go back and read this chapter as it is really easy to drift away from preparing for key elements of your practice.

Check list

	Tick
I have:	
◦ read the key Department for Education documentation on Safeguarding and Child Protection;	
◦ read the school's Safeguarding and Child Protection policies and know the name of the safeguarding lead in the school;	
◦ read the school behaviour policy;	
◦ discussed the school and class rules with the class;	
◦ read the school marking policy;	
◦ thought about what might be a challenge in terms of my pedagogical or subject knowledge and have organised to observe other teachers.	
I know:	
◦ the special needs of some children in my class;	
◦ children for whom English is an additional language.	

Further suggestions

- Key documents for Safeguarding and Child Protection are regularly updated, so make sure you read the latest versions

Check to see whether your institution or placement school is a member of:

- Nasen—the National Association of special educational needs (nasen.org.uk);
- Naldic—the National Subject Association for teaching EAL (naldic.org.uk).

CHAPTER 5

Knowing the children and pupil progress

This chapter should help you to:

- get to know the children:
    - as individuals
    - as learners;
- focus on pupil progress:
    - using data and assessment tools within the school
    - assessment for learning
    - evidence of progress;
- understand language of report writing.

Introduction

In previous school placements, you will have been developing your skills and knowledge of teaching and learning and of course you will have focused on pupil progress. In the final placement, you must develop a much sharper focus on the progress of all the children in your class. In meeting with your class teacher and mentor you should be able to talk about and provide evidence of the children's progress. This chapter should help you to ensure that you are prepared for this aspect of your practice from the start of final placement

Knowing the children as individuals

Knowing the class of children as individuals and building a class community is something that is key when you have your first class. This will be addressed in detail in the final section of the book. On your final placement, you will be with the children for a fairly long time and teaching the class for the vast majority of the time, so it is important to understand your role in making the children feel valued as individuals. When a learner feels valued, they are far more likely to make progress.

Greetings at the beginning of the day

You will be mirroring the routines of the class teacher at the beginning of the placement but making sure that you:

- make eye contact with every child at the beginning of every day;
- take time during the register to greet every child.

Having a personal greeting is so important in setting a positive atmosphere for learning as well as teaching the children social skills. Every day should be a new beginning for the children.

Name cards

It is useful to get the children to make name cards that can sit on their desks facing you at the front of the class. You will then be able to start using all the names in any interactions.

"Billy, you've got your hand up so I am going to let you answer this question."
"Excellent Yamini, I can see you are ready to start learning."

The children can then draw something they like doing on the other side of the name card. As time goes on you may be able to use some of these interests in your teaching.

"Today for our counting we are going to use dogs to count as I know Ben loves dogs."
"Josefa, I know you love singing, so in our music lesson you can choose a song for us to sing at the end of the lesson."

Test yourself after the first week of placement by trying to remember all the names of the children in the class. Find out which children you have missed and ensure you get to know them the following week.

Knowing the children as learners

Allow yourself some time to observe the children in different learning situations as well as playtimes. It is time well spent at the beginning of your final placement.

Notice the children who:	You will need to:
cannot sit still for long;	■ plan for movement in some learning opportunities;
answer before thinking;	■ make sure the children have 'thinking time' with hands in their laps rather than hands up;

Notice the children who:	You will need to:
want to answer every question;	■ include partner talk so everyone has a voice and is actively involved in learning opportunities;
do not like to answer in class situations;	■ use partner talk so that the children can develop their confidence, pre warn a child that you will be asking them a particular question (they can always ask their partner for help);
are slow to get started on learning tasks;	■ break down the information into smaller chunks;
might misbehave if seated together;	■ adhere to careful seating arrangements, places on the carpet and talking partners/learning partners that the teacher has already arranged;
shine in different areas of the curriculum;	■ ensure that you notice and celebrate their achievements;
always finish first;	■ introduce 'self-reflection' strategies to enable the child to focus on the depth of their learning; ■ ensure you have an open-ended learning activity;
lose concentration quickly.	■ give shorter learning activities; ■ highlight the time required for each learning activity; ■ include mini plenaries to refocus learning.

Continue to make notes of your observations and think about the implications for you as a teacher. This will be much easier to achieve when observing as opposed to when you are fully engaged with teaching the whole class.

Pupil progress—using data and assessment tools within the school

Teaching trainee teachers about school data has become more complex over the last few years as schools have increasingly adopted their own systems for collecting and analysing data. This therefore means that trainee teachers have to understand the different methods of data collection and recording systems wherever they are in placement. The systems and recording of data collection may be different but the purpose remains the same: data should be used to understand the progress and attainment of children and whether the teaching and learning opportunities enable all children to make progress. Getting involved with data collection is key to understanding how to prepare for data collection points throughout the year so that they do not become stressful when you have your own class.

When there are so many things to think about when starting your final placement, looking at available class data may not be top of your list of things to do. It will become a focal point of discussions with your line manager, mentor, or headteacher when you have your own class. Data raises questions about the most appropriate provision for some children, for example, whether an intervention group is appropriate.

On final placement try to:

- visit and if possible get involved in an intervention group;
- speak to the SENCO/Inclusion manager and observe/get involved in some focused teaching;
- observe a speech therapist or anyone else visiting the school with specific knowledge/skills.

Ask how information on progress and attainment is relayed back to the class teacher and how the class teacher can support the learning undertaken in these sessions. Any intervention group should not be a stand-alone learning opportunity: there are always ways to develop the knowledge, understanding, and skills developed in these sessions into learning opportunities in the classroom and around the school environment. It will be unlikely that you will ever have an opportunity to observe and take part in these different focus groups sessions to such an extent once you become a qualified teacher, so do make the most of any opportunities.

Ask to meet with the assessment lead at the beginning of your final placement in order to look at pupil progress and attainment data on the children you will be teaching. The type of data collected depends on the age of the children.

Firstly, look at the data with the school assessment lead.

Possible questions to ask:

- How and when is the data collected?
- What does the data tell you?
- What questions does the data raise?
- How can a class teacher prepare for data collection?

Secondly, ask whether you can get involved in the collection of class progress/attainment data and whether you can input information onto the school's system (the assessment lead may want you to do this with your class teacher initially).

Thirdly, think about how the analysis of data might impact on teaching and learning opportunities.

Pupil progress—assessment for learning

Embedding assessment for learning opportunities into your daily teaching is such an important element of your practice to develop. Trainee teachers are on a journey that initially starts with the 'survival' stage of standing in front of a class of children, managing behaviour whilst developing the skill of teaching. Over time the focus should gradually shift to the understanding that teaching is about the progress of the learner and responding to their needs. Assessment for learning is the active engagement of the teacher in responding to the needs of the learner in a lesson and the active engagement of the learner in improving their learning.

How to get started on assessment for learning

Trainee teachers can sometimes find embedding assessment for learning strategies into their teaching a challenge, so here are some approaches and examples to help you get started. The examples will need to be adapted according to the age of the children you will be teaching. I have used the term learning question in the following examples; you may be used to learning intention, learning objective, or other terms. Whatever term you use, children need to have a clear idea of what they are trying to learn, so make the learning question clear. Later on in your teaching career, you can develop an understanding that you do not always have to start with a learning question, but it is probably easier for most trainee teachers to start with this approach as it helps to keep your teaching focused. Keep the learning question simple.

Example 1—Using the learning question and success criteria

Learning question:

'Can I be more descriptive in my writing?'

Success criteria:

- include an opening sentence that 'hooks' the reader;
- use adjectives to describe the character.

As a trainee teacher you can start off by giving the children the success criteria but as you become more confident you can ask the children what the success criteria might be.

After the initial input at the beginning of the lesson, where you might have explored great opening sentences in fiction books, give the children 10 minutes to compose an opening sentence that 'hooks' the reader. Get the children to share their sentences with a partner and ask how the sentences could be even better. Give the children time to write their improved sentence. Share a couple of examples with the class to model how opening sentences have improved.

Provide some teacher input on character description using adjectives. Model how you draft your writing, then take ideas from the children to make your writing even better. Now give the children time to describe their character using adjectives.

After 15 minutes ask the children to stop writing and to underline all the adjectives in their writing in a coloured pencil. Get the children to check with their partner if they have underlined adjectives and get them to read their character descriptions to a partner. Did the adjectives help the partner create a picture of the character in their head? How could the writing be improved? The children get feedback from their partner and redraft. Ensure the children know that writers draft their work. This is a 'real life' process.

This example is AfL in action. You will have evidence of how learning has improved. The children might not have written much but this approach has the potential to impact on the quality of the written work.

AfL opportunities allow learning to be 'chunked'.

Example 2—adding to the success criteria

Learning question

'Can I create a gymnastic sequence with a partner?'

Success criteria

The sequence must include:

- mirroring with my partner;
- 1 symmetrical shape;
- 1 asymmetrical shape.

After some teacher input and learner activity on mirroring and symmetrical and asymmetrical shapes, explain the learning question as well as the success criteria. It is useful to have the success criteria written out on a large piece of paper that you can put on the wall and refer to it in the lesson.
After 10 minutes, 2 pairs join together. Each pair demonstrates what they have created so far. They then give each other feedback.
One pair says, "*We can't give them any feedback as they have everything in the success criteria.*" This is a teaching opportunity where you can ask the class what could be added to the success criteria.

Added success criteria:

- Mirroring must include different levels.

A further 10 minutes is spent developing and refining the gymnastic sequence. The groups join together again to demonstrate how they have improved their gymnastic sequence.

This example is AfL in action. The children should have produced higher quality gymnastic sequences after having feedback. As a teacher you get involved in the feedback and model clear points for improvement. It takes children time to learn how to give and receive feedback from their peers, but even 5 year olds can start to develop this skill.

> *If, as teachers, we do not respond to the progress of learners we are putting a ceiling on our expectations or ignoring the learning needs of children.*

Example 3—Adjusting learning opportunities in lessons and at the end of lessons

AfL is about personalising learning opportunities to meet the needs of the learners. Trainee teachers may get feedback from the children in the lesson by asking them to respond with thumbs up, down, or midway as a means of finding out whether the children understand. However, the most important thing to do when some children have clearly stated that they do not understand is to adapt your teaching accordingly. Create a focus group and spend an extra few minutes teaching this group. Unplanned focus groups can be set up at any point in a lesson according to the needs of the learners. Similarly, at the end of the lesson or when marking, you know that some children have still not been able to answer the learning question positively or with confidence. You may have asked them to feedback to you in their books with a symbol to demonstrate their level of understanding. You will now need to adapt your next lesson to meet their learning needs. Do you need to start the next lesson with a whole class input or can you start the lesson by giving the class a challenge? In this time, you can teach a focus group.

Learners who are constantly getting everything 'right' need to be challenged and need to understand that struggling is part of learning so you also need to adapt learning opportunities for these children. It is impossible to always plan for and predict the exact needs of all the children in your class prior to the lesson but you can adapt your teaching during a lesson. Being flexible and adapting to the needs of the learners should help with behaviour as children should be engaging in learning at the appropriate level of challenge.

Adapt teaching to meet the needs of the learners.

Example 4—Questioning and interactions

Well thought out questions at the planning stage should help you with your teaching and provide you with information about:

- what children are learning;
- how the children are thinking;
- misconceptions.

You then need to respond and adapt your teaching according to the answers you receive.
For example:

Teacher: *"Who do you think is the hero in the story?"*
Child: *"Jack."*
Teacher: *"Well done."*

This is an example of low-level questioning that does not delve deeply into the child's understanding. The following example demonstrates how a teacher can really find out the depth of the child's understanding:

Teacher: *"Who do you think is the hero of the story?"*
Child: *"Jack."*
Teacher: *"Why do you think Jack is the hero?"*
Child: *"Because it says here that Jack was brave to climb the beanstalk."*
Teacher: *"Are there any more clues to tell us that Jack was brave?"*

Note how in this response the child has to justify their answer. If a child gives an incorrect answer do not just say no that's not right or move on too quickly to a child who can give you the correct answer. Ask the child how they came to get the answer, this may give you information so you can adapt your teaching to help the child. Misconceptions are an important aspect of learning.

Child: *"I think the circuit is going to work."*
Teacher: *"No, it's not going to work because it's not a complete circuit."*

In this example the child has not been given an opportunity to think through why the circuit is not working.

Child: *"I think the circuit is going to work."*

Teacher: *"Let's see if it does."*
Child: *"No, it's not working."*
Teacher: *"O.K. talk me through the journey of the electricity in the circuit."*
Child: *"Oh yes, here the circuit is broken so the electricity can't get around."*

This example is telling the teacher far more about what the child knows and understands. It is also allowing the child to respond to the teacher's interaction, giving them time to think and make progress.

Develop your questioning technique and the quality of your interactions in order to learn about children's thinking and understanding.

Pupil progress—evidence of progress

Evidence of progress of children's learning is usually a key feature of the final placement. The type of evidence can depend on:

- the type of learning you are trying to evidence;
- providing opportunities that allow the children to demonstrate what they have learnt.

Types of evidence	Ways to demonstrate progress	Further notes
Responses to your marking or to peer feedback	3 pieces of evidence where the children have responded to marking to improve their learning	Children must be given time to respond to marking.
Annotations on pieces of work	Trainee teacher annotates evidence of learning and next steps. Children respond to marking.	The annotations provide context and additional information.
Photographs	Photographs can be taken at the beginning of a sequence of learning and then at the end, e.g. circuits in science.	The children can annotate the photographs or the trainee teacher can.
Filming	Film the first gymnastic sequence on shape and then film the last sequence.	Get the children to review their own progress.

Types of evidence	Ways to demonstrate progress	Further notes
Mind mapping	Make a mind map at the beginning of a topic and then do the same at the end of the topic.	The mind map can take different forms, e.g. it can be written or drawn.
Trainee teacher as scribe or observer of learning	Trainee teacher can observe groups of children at the beginning of a new sequence of learning and then at the end.	Early years practitioners are experts in observing and making notes on progress. Spend an afternoon observing them collecting evidence.
Digital recorder	Children can record their learning, e.g. recording a radio programme for another year group on World War 2 evacuees.	Think of alternatives to written evidence.

There are many ways to provide evidence of progress including many computer programs that are especially designed for this purpose. Explore what is available in your school. Right at the beginning of the final placement, think about how and when you can evidence the progress of the learners that you teach. Wherever possible allow the children to be active in understanding how evidence of learning can be captured. Doing this in different ways can be motivating. Make learning the key topic of conversation.

Keep the language of learning at the heart of your teaching.

What have we learnt today?

The language of report writing

Writing reports for your first class can be a stressful time. There are strategies that you can use to make this a far less stressful time (this will be addressed in the final part of the book). I must highlight how it is a really good idea to have some practice on the final placement. In the final 2 or 3 weeks of placement you should be thinking about writing reports for about 6 children. Yes, you will be tired but this will be time well spent.

End of year reports are nearly always kept by families and brought out occasionally for many years to come. It is fascinating looking at reports of famous people and seeing whether the essence of the person was really captured by their teacher. Reports are important documents and as teachers we should be truthful as well as being mindful about choosing our words carefully.

Each school has their own systems for report writing. Ask if you can use the school system at your final placement as a template. A suggestion is that you look at a few excellent examples first as this really helps to model the approach required.

Look up the report for a child from another class who:

- has challenging behaviour;
- has a special educational need;
- is a high attainer.

Analyse the:

- language that is used in the report;
- ways in which attainment and progress are reported;
- ways in which the language of learning and targets/next steps are clear and concise.

Now try to write your 6 reports trying to mirror the excellent examples you analysed. Ask your class teacher if he/she can recognise the learner from the report. Ask for feedback on the reports you found more challenging to write. This will be time well spent.

Summary

On final placement, get involved with understanding any data on the children as soon as possible. Find out how and when the data is collected and what implications this information has for teaching and learning. Data can be really useful in helping to understand the needs and progress of children as well as thinking about the different learning opportunities we provide as teachers in order to help all children make progress. Be careful not to label children and put a ceiling on your expectations. It is very easy to put children into certain 'attainment groups' and plan for these groups based purely on data. Children can become 'stuck' in these groups if we are not adaptable. This is where the skill of teaching can really come into play, adapting to how children are responding to different learning opportunities within a lesson and being flexible with your expectations. Assessment for learning opportunities really allows for you as a teacher to understand the progress of children as well as helping them to take ownership of their learning. Make AfL opportunities an integral part of every lesson and focus on the language of learning. What have we learnt?

Check list

	Tick
I greet every child every morning;	
I embed AfL strategies into my teaching;	
I adapt my planning/teaching according to the learning needs of the children in response to assessment;	
I understand the data for pupil progress/attainment;	
I can plan for data collection and input data on the school's system.;	
I have: ◦ collected evidence of children's progress;	
◦ looked at excellent examples of report writing;	
◦ written 6 reports and got feedback.	

PART 2

The transition phase
The transition from training to your first job as a primary school teacher

CHAPTER 6

Building upon and developing new relationships

This chapter should help you to:

- understand the importance of the support links with your:
  - training provider
  - friends/peers from your training provider
  - local networks;
- develop professional relationships with the:
  - headteacher
  - mentor
  - other teachers
  - TA
  - parents/carers.

Introduction

There is a real tendency to think about your training and starting your new post in teaching as 2 very separate entities: this chapter should help to bridge the gap between the 2. The chapter should also help you to build on the support network that has helped you so far in your training to be a teacher as well as thinking about how you need to develop the new network of professional relationships.

The importance of support links

Training provider

Once you have passed your final school placement it is very easy to separate yourself from your training provider and get on with your new job as a teacher. On whichever pathway you are being trained, your provider will have thought very carefully about the transition stage after final placement. Lectures, visiting speakers, or group seminars will have been arranged specifically for your needs, with perhaps an NQT guest speaker who has undergone your training speaking to you about their experiences of their first year in teaching. These sessions are absolutely invaluable, so please make sure you make the most of whatever has been organised for you. There should be a programme for newly qualified teachers at your first teaching post, but you may have little opportunity initially to attend any additional courses for your continual professional development, so any provision by your training provider should be taken advantage of.

You might be offered an opportunity to start working the last few weeks of term at the school in which you have gained your first teaching post. This can be very tempting but think carefully about the pros and cons of doing this. It is always worthwhile getting some experience of the school in which you will be working but you will also need time to re-charge your energy levels. If the school has a particular INSET day on introducing a new way of working in a particular subject, this would definitely be worth attending. Do speak to someone from your training provider for any advice with these sorts of issues.

People from your training provider will have spent years teaching, working with training and educating teachers of the future, and developing a deep understanding of the world of education, so make sure you keep these important links. Over the years, newly qualified teachers whom I have taught have sent amazing messages about how they are getting on in their new role. If permission is granted, these messages can be shared with the current cohort of trainee teachers to inspire them. It has been a real privilege to witness the careers of those I have taught, with some former trainees coming back to lead lectures or seminars as newly qualified teachers, year leaders, or even headteachers. Keeping in touch with your training provider can also help you with decisions you may wish to make about aspects of your career such as pursuing Masters credits, getting involved with some lecturing, or, in time, becoming a mentor for trainee teachers on school placements. There have been many times when those I have taught in the past have sought advice about career choices.

Many training providers have conferences, twilight drop-in sessions, or online support for newly qualified teachers, so do keep in touch and try to attend these sessions. It is always positive to spend some time with other early career teachers and to continue to build a support network. You do not often have enough time to reflect in depth when you start teaching, so do take up any opportunities you can when they are offered. Attending a drop-in session or a seminar at the place where you trained is personal for you as the sessions are likely to be run by people that you know. The conversations and discussions should be building on trust that developed when you were training and you can perhaps be more open and honest about the challenges that you face.

Trainee teachers who attend university courses have a library on site but almost all trainees, regardless of their training route, should have access to a university library. Often these libraries have significant teaching resources with a specialised librarian. This person usually holds a wealth of knowledge and is there to help you. When you get offered your first job, you may well be still officially linked to your training institution so you should still be able to use these facilities. If you know that you are going to be teaching a particular topic in History, for example, go and research. Or maybe the class you will be teaching presents with some challenging behaviour so go and spend a day looking through resources or books that you will find really useful. Just being in a quiet space that is full of resources may be inspiring and help develop your confidence.

Friends and peers from your training provider

The relationships that you build up with those that you train with can never be underestimated. There will probably be people who you will be in contact with and potentially be friends with for many years to come, if not for life. I know that the friend I met on the third day of my undergraduate teaching course has been my life-long friend. We have had endless conversations about teaching and learning and have been a support for each other throughout our very long careers. These trusting relationships are so important as they grow and develop along with your teaching experiences over time. When I started my first job, I had the hardest and most demanding class I have ever taught but my friend was always there to listen to my concerns. This class turned out to be the best and most creative class ever and I learnt so much from them; that was the start of an amazingly fulfilling career.

My friend and I have always communicated via the phone, even though we could email, text, and use various other means of contact. Nowadays you have many different forms of communicating but as mentioned in the first part of this book, never use the name of the school, anyone you work with, or any child in any written form of communication outside of school documentation, even if the form of communication is not in the public domain.

Local networks

When you get your first job or even perhaps in the interview you need to be finding out about what support is available for newly qualified teachers in the school. Your school may be linked to a local authority, a trust, or another organisation. These organisations should run courses for NQTS and there may even be a course that you could attend prior to starting your first teaching post. This would provide you with a further opportunity to start building a network with other NQTs in the local area. If your school is in a cluster of local schools that meet regularly for support and training, see whether there is specific support for NQTs. If there are any local authority, trust, or cluster school opportunities for NQTs, do get involved.

Developing professional relationships

Headteacher

The headteacher is someone who will want to make sure that you feel welcome in the school and that you receive all the necessary support and mentoring as a newly qualified teacher. They are also your assessor, so you need to ensure interactions, including written communication, are fairly formal in nature. Your mentor and year leader, rather than the headteacher, will usually be your main points of contact, especially in large schools, but your headteacher should be someone that you can approach and ask for advice and support.

Mentor

Your mentor is usually the deputy headteacher or someone in a senior position within the school. This is the person who you should particularly build up a trusting relationship with; they should guide you, be approachable, and ensure that you develop as a teacher and a colleague in the community of the school. A trusting relationship is built up over time: it is built on the mentor having the necessary interpersonal skills for this role, but a trusting relationship is also built on the mentee understanding their role. From the outset, you will need to demonstrate that you are organised by asking for:

- key documentation (safeguarding and child protection, behaviour, assessment, marking, staff behaviour policy);
- the outline of the NQT support for the year;
- the pattern of observations (not exact dates).

If your job starts in September, ask your mentor if you can take photographs of the classroom that you will be teaching in before the end of the summer term. This will give you an idea of how the classroom is currently set out, rather than discovering an empty room with furniture stacked in the corner of the classroom during the summer holidays. Also, it is worthwhile asking your mentor if you can observe the class you will be teaching as they may well have rules and routines that work particularly well and would be worthwhile mirroring in the new term. Planning in advance should demonstrate to your mentor that you are organised and thinking ahead.

You will also need to know when you can come into the school and set up your classroom. There is a whole chapter dedicated to this, but setting up your class takes time, so this will need to be arranged in advance. Schools usually have set weeks when the school is open in holiday time, but you need to also ensure that there are people like your mentor or year leader around for some of the time to help you with key information. It can be quite daunting to come into school when there is nobody to show you where everything is.

The role of mentor is interesting as they should be a support and should provide challenge in developing your practice but can also be one of your assessors. Always be mindful of the gentle building of this professional relationship. Have an open heart and mind in terms of your personal journey as a teacher; a person who is always learning.

Other teachers

The other teachers in the school will be so important to you. If you have a year group leader, they will be a key point of contact, as they will be able to help you with the planning for the term ahead and will be aware of all the resources available in the school. You will need to meet with this teacher and potentially the rest of the year group team to plan for the term ahead. You will need to know how this planning translates into weekly planning, when this is done, and how it is done. Looking at some previous plans and knowing when the planning will be taking place should develop your confidence. Also, this is a time to find out whether subjects are taught in a particular way and you may find that observing some subjects being taught beneficial. Most probably everything will be new to you but if you can bring a few ideas to any planning meeting, the teachers that you will be working with will start to believe that you are a team player who is able and willing to contribute ideas.

The SENCO/Inclusion manager is a key person to meet if you know that you have children in your new class with special needs. Do not just rely on a child being given a 'label'; find out about the individual needs of the child and how this translates into their learning needs. You may be able to find out if these children are involved in intervention groups and how this then affects your planning. In addition, these children will have specific targets so begin to think about how you can incorporate these into everyday teaching and learning situations.

Find out about:

- review and target setting points in the year;
- meetings with parents/carers.

Put these on a timeline for the year.

The assessment lead in the school is also a key person to meet, but your year group leader will also be able to help you with understanding how your year group plans for assessment points. You need to have information about what and how assessment information is collected throughout the year. Collecting, inputting, and analysing data can seem daunting to begin with but you should always have people to help you at every stage.

Find out about:

- key assessment points in the year;
- how assessment data is collected.

Put these on a timeline for the year.

Teaching assistant (TA)

If you have a teaching assistant, it is always worth trying to meet them before the start of the new term as they may feel anxious working with a new teacher in the school. Usually, a more experienced TA is teamed up with a newly qualified teacher. This relationship is important as you will be working with each other on a daily basis. It may feel as though the TA is more experienced than you and they will certainly know the routines of the school and probably know the children well. Do remember that you are the professional lead in the classroom, so tact and careful consideration of the roles is required. It is worthwhile talking to the previous class teacher that worked with the TA and ask about the routines, roles, and responsibilities that the TA undertook in the previous academic year, as well as areas of the curriculum where they feel particularly confident in supporting children's learning. At this stage, in the early days of meeting each other, just make it known that you are really looking forward to working with him/her. Try to use inclusive language, such as "*our class*" whenever possible. TAs are usually paid during term time only so be careful about asking if they can come in to help set up the classroom during the summer holidays.

A card for your TA stating how much you are looking forward to working with him/her would be well received. Again, it is these little touches that make all the difference in building the working relationship of someone who wants to work with you as opposed to having to work with you.

Parents/carers

You always need to take guidance from your mentor about sending any written messages to parents/carers and usually messages are checked before being sent. If your mentor allows you to send a message, this is a good way to briefly introduce yourself and let it be known how much you are looking forward to teaching at the school. Here is an example of the tone of the correspondence required.

Dear Parents/Carers of Year 3, I would like to take this opportunity of introducing myself as the new teacher of Badger Class from September. I met with the class this week and they told me all about the things they are looking forward to next term.

> *Just to let you know that I will be based in Badger class at the open evening on July 5th. I look forward to meeting as many of you as possible then. If you are unable to attend, I will look forward to seeing you in September.*
>
> *Kind regards,*

If you do get the chance to meet parents/carers before the summer holidays, do take a note book. You will probably be given lots of information and it may be really pertinent and important for you to remember. Do not make any comments or get involved in discussions such as being told that a child has not had a good year or has not made great progress. Also do not make any promises, such as where you will seat a child. A brief comment such as "*Oh, I haven't thought about any of that yet*" should suffice. Do try to speak to as many people as possible and try to speak to those who may be a little more reticent in coming forward to speak to you. If you have met the children already and have found out something about them, you might be able to use some of this information in conversation.

If a parent/carer is particularly worried about something, such as the new teacher understanding their child's special need, do put their mind at rest by telling them that you will meet with them at the beginning of term, hopefully with the SENCO/Inclusion manager. There may even be an opportunity to be involved in review meetings at the end of the term before you start your new job.

Trust—building relationships

Relationships are built on trust. School leadership, teachers, support staff, parents/carers, children, and anyone involved in the community of school need to know that the new teacher in their community can be trusted and that they have the ability to build up positive professional relationships with everyone in their community.

All throughout my career, the colleagues who have been the most respected are those who have integrity and do not have negative words to say about others. They know the key people they need to discuss professional issues with and always ensure words are chosen carefully. Human nature is such that there will always be individuals who are more negative than others, whatever profession you are in. Getting involved in 'gossip' and less professional conversations are easy to slip into when trying to develop new relationships with colleagues: my advice would be to not get involved as they will not be good for your wellbeing and your standing in the school community. People soon know not to involve you in unnecessary discussions if you do not contribute. At the transition stage of becoming a teacher, you are more likely to be meeting with staff you will be working with in the school holidays, when everyone is more relaxed. Just be mindful that you are at the beginning stage of building up these important relationships that must be professional. Surround yourself with positive influences whenever possible.

Go back to the first part of the book (Chapter 2) to remind yourself of the importance of how you communicate with colleagues: remind yourself that you are in a working environment and that all forms of communication should remain professional. Always think that any form of communication could be seen by anyone. This really makes you think about what and how you write. Remember that you must never use the school name or names of colleagues or children in any communication.

When you are setting up your classroom in the holidays, even though you think you might not be able to spare the time, if colleagues ask you out for lunch, do go. It is important to understand that these colleagues will form part of your support network, and these professional relationships need to be gradually developed. Try not to just feel comfortable with 1 or 2 people in the school, visit other classrooms when teachers are getting prepared in the holidays and have a chat. You may find that you start to build up a network of support across the school.

Summary

The importance of relationships and how to approach the different layers of relationships in which you have to engage in the community of school is really hard to teach. Keep the word 'professional' in your head in all your interactions, whilst still presenting as approachable and friendly. Using the following check list will enable you to organise the collection of different information from a range of people, rather than asking your mentor to organise meetings for you. If you check with your mentor that this is alright to do, they will probably view you as someone who is proactive in getting the information you need as well as building up the different relationships necessary in the school environment.

Check list

Be mindful that some of this information may not be available until the start of the new term.

	Tick
I have met with my mentor and have: ∘ an outline of the NQT programme;	
∘ key policies (safeguarding, behaviour, marking, assessment, staff behaviour policy).	

	Tick
I have met with my year/phase leader and have: ◦ an outline of the term's planning;	
◦ timetable;	
◦ date of class assembly;	
◦ date of parent/carer consultations;	
◦ date of Christmas production.	
I have met with the SENCO/Inclusion manager and have: ◦ key information of children in my class with special needs.	
◦ dates of review meetings.	
I have met with the assessment leader and have: ◦ key assessment points in the Autumn term;	
◦ class data useful when planning for the Autumn term.	
I am aware of the support (twilight sessions, conferences, drop-in sessions) from my training provider.	

CHAPTER 7

Getting to know your future class

This chapter should help you to:

- understand the importance of the first meeting with your class, with a focus on:
  - a shared understanding of class rules
  - building a sense of community;
- know what information to collect from the current class teacher.

Introduction

This chapter assumes that you will be starting your first teaching post in the September of the Autumn term, but if this is not the case the information provided in this chapter is still relevant. This is the really exciting time, as at long last, you will get to meet the children you are going to be teaching. This chapter should help you to prepare for the first meeting with your future class, which usually takes place at the end of the summer term, with some ideas of what you should be hoping to achieve in this first meeting.

First meeting with your class

The way in which the children enter and leave the classroom is so important on the first meeting. Make sure the children do not rush into or out of the new learning space. Line the children up if necessary and give clear instructions as to where you want them to sit. Equally, when leaving the classroom, ensure that you think this through carefully. You are setting the foundations for the routines that you will use throughout the next academic year. The consistent use of these routines cannot be underestimated for smooth transitions.

My suggestion for this first meeting is to either develop:

- a shared understanding of class rules; or
- an understanding of the class as a community.

Both of these are important so whichever you do not choose you should address at the start of the new term.

The children need to know that you are approachable and that you are really looking forward to teaching them for the next school year. They also need to know that you are confident and in control. The class should leave for the summer holidays looking forward to coming into their new class in September and working with their new teacher.

A shared understanding of class rules—first lesson ideas

It is so important to set up your class rules, class agreement, or charter. You will have read the school behaviour policy so now this needs to be translated into a shared understanding with the class. A good way to start the lesson might be:

Example 1

"In September we will all be in Squirrel class. What can we all agree to do that will make our classroom a safe and happy place to learn?"

This approach is straight forward and useful for younger primary children. In most schools the classes have names; make sure you use the name to highlight the identity of the class. The children should come up with lots of ideas such as:

- do not shout out;
- do not talk when others are talking;
- do not say nasty things.

You now need to manage the discussion so that you and the children agree on about 3 key rules. Change them from a negative statement to a positive statement.
In Squirrel class we:

- put our hands up when we want to answer;
- listen to others;
- are kind.

The children can then be given a round piece of paper divided into 3 sections, with their name in the middle. They can draw a picture related to each rule. You could also have some children in role play to show what each rule might 'look like' in their classroom; take a photograph and add captions. Make sure you and your TA and any regular additional support in the classroom have your own circle and photograph, so you can also model expectations to the children. This can then be used as your first display to be put up over the summer holidays ready for you to refer to at times when the children are putting their hand up, listening, and using kind words, as well as when you need to remind children of the rules. The circles of names and pictures can form 1 big circle with the 3 rules in the middle.

Example 2

"You are all going to be top of the school in Year 6. What do you think are the most important things that we should agree on that will help you achieve your best?"

This question should spark discussion or you will need to guide a discussion on the importance of looking after each other, respecting each other, and everyone helping each other to achieve their very best. If you find yourself in a Year 6 class, there is often the temptation to focus on achieving certain results at the end of the year. This may dominate the discussion, as it is something the children may be worried about. If this is the case, try to change the focus towards the effort each child makes in order to reach their own personal goal. A goal does not have to be a number but a set of success criteria that the children can aim for. The children then have more of an idea of the goal they are trying to reach. This approach is more likely to have a positive effect on the morale of the class, placing value on effort as well as valuing the outcome of all learners. It also places the focus away from possible competition and more about the effort of each individual.

With Year 6, you can discuss the importance of creating a positive learning atmosphere. You can provide examples on how in the world of work, people rarely work alone but rely on the skills, knowledge, expertise, and commitment of others. Even with adults there are rules in the work place, such as having a Chair Person to run a meeting to ensure that everyone gets heard. With the children you can then guide the discussion to making links between the world of work and key rules that are needed in the classroom. With older children in a primary school you might want to call it a class agreement or a charter. There are many different ways to display class agreements, but try to phrase the agreement in a positive way and display it prominently where it can be referred to when necessary.

Using circular shaped paper with the agreed rules in the middle, older children in a primary school might like to draw their ambitions for a future career around the circle. These are always useful to refer to during the school year when looking at why certain things have to be learnt. I remember a time when an aspiring footballer in my class asked why he needed to learn about decimals and percentages. We had an interesting discussion about contracts, earnings, and tax! Another idea for slightly younger children is for the pictures on the class agreement to be about the children themselves: what they like doing, what pets they have, and what subjects they love. You can then use this information at different points throughout the school year. Whatever the age of the children, make sure all adults are visually represented in the same way on the display. The children may leave this first lesson knowing that their teacher loves singing, reading, and playing rugby. They may find out that their TA likes to go to the cinema, dancing, and cooking.

Other examples of visually representing class rules can be:

- drawing around hands, cutting them out, and decorating and display as a circle of joined hands or fix onto a large hoop;
- names of the children in shapes that fit together in a tessellation;
- a branch of a tree in a pot with the rules stuck onto either the pot or the trunk, with children's names and pictures hanging from the branches.

Make the rules, charter, or class agreement clear so that you can refer to them.

Building a sense of community—first lesson ideas

Developing an understanding as a class as a community of learners is another idea that you can use in the first lesson with your future class. A sense of community in a classroom setting can be achieved by:

- feeling that you belong and are valued;
- understanding the needs of others;
- contributing to your community.

There will be more in Part 3 of this book about building relationships and community but right from the start, from your first meeting with the children, you can begin to develop an understanding. This will need to be presented in a visual way to show the importance of being an individual and that many individuals make up the community of the class. Each of the following ideas needs to be preceded with a discussion on the meaning of community in the classroom. The following are examples of ways of visually representing the ideas the children come up with.

Example 1—Brick wall

Explore the importance of being an individual and how boring it would be if we were all the same. Give the children a piece of paper the size of the side of a brick and get the children to draw everything that makes them special or unique.

Explain to the children that the bricks decorated with pictures are going to be a display of a strong wall. The strong wall is the community of learners and each brick is the individual learner. Explore what is needed to link all the bricks together.

"What is the glue that links us all together as a community of learners?"

Once the wall of bricks is displayed, the mortar or glue can contain key words that have been agreed with the class, such as respect and kindness.

Example 2—Model

The children can make a model or a 3D picture of something that represents them. These can then be added to a 3D class column. This column then represents 1 class made up of many individuals.

Example 3—Class logo

A discussion can ensue on the key elements of what will make their class a community of learners, a positive environment in which to learn, to help each other, and to strive to reach personal as well as class goals. After looking at some inspiring logos and how they convey meaning, a class logo can be designed.

Example 4—Class song, rhyme, or poem

A class rap, poem, or song can be created to depict the community of the class. You may want to use a simple existing song, poem, or rhyme as a basis for writing something new.

The rhythm of Humpty Dumpty can be used to create a new rhyme.

Humpty Dumpty sat on a wall,	Squirrel class are as good as can be,
Humpty Dumpty had a great fall,	Squirrel class are great company,
All the King's horses and all the King's men,	All of the children and all of the staff,
Couldn't put Humpty together again.	All learn together and have a great laugh.

Do not worry if you do not finish what you started in the introductory lesson with the class as it can be completed at a later date.

In this first lesson with your future class, you will also need to be aware of the worries that some children may have. Many children are unsettled by change and we do not often think of the little things that make children worried such as:

- moving from Key Stage 1 to Key Stage 2 where the playground might be different with bigger children;

- where lunch boxes are left in the morning;
- where coats are left.

Before the introductory lesson with your future class, the current teacher could have relayed information to you about all the things the children are looking forward to and all the things that they are worried about. You might then be able to alleviate some of these fears in your introductory lesson.

Getting key information from the class teacher

As I mentioned at the beginning of this part of the book, my first class were really challenging. They had quite a few teachers in the previous year and, on the day of my interview, the class teacher said she was leaving teaching because of the class. I did not meet that teacher again and, in many ways, I was glad because I am not sure I would have heard too many positive comments. Yes, the class was challenging, especially in the Autumn term, but I learnt so much from them and I was really sorry to see them go into Year 6 at the end of the academic year. I wonder whether the class just got a reputation that got passed from teacher to teacher and the 'hand overs' between teachers were full of negative comments. I also wonder if I might not have been so successful with the class if I had heard too many negative comments about them. This is why it is good to think of a strategy about what and how information is relayed from teacher to teacher. You can therefore be proactive in the ways in which you ask for information.

Important and useful information can be relayed from teacher to teacher, such as children who have a history of not getting on with each other so that you will be careful about where they are seated. Do be wary if labels have already been put on children, such as the 'naughty child' or the 'average child'. Try as hard as you can to not hold onto these labels, as this is likely to impact on your reactions to and expectations of individual children. What is important to find out is the strategies that will help a child if they sometimes present with challenging behaviours. If, like my first class, you have a class with many emotional and social needs, you need to discuss positive strategies for helping the children. Make sure you make notes to remind you of this key information with the heading 'positive strategies' so if you are given negative information, turn it around and ask what are the best ways in which to help the child. Also ask what the child is good at.

A new class should be a new start.

With regards to parents/carers you may well hear of some who are trickier than others. It is very easy to say, but try not to dwell on this information.

Throughout my career, there have been a very small minority of parents/carers who have been really challenging. These are also the ones that you remember, as opposed to the vast majority who are pleased with the education their child receives. In my experience, when parents/carers were challenging it was because school had not been a positive aspect of their lives or for some reason they were particularly worried about their child. There is almost always a reason why a parent/carer reacts in a certain way. Also, sometimes as teachers we do not always get it right and sometimes being challenged can make us think about our practice. So again, seek information about strategies to work in partnership with these parents/carers and how to build up a positive relationship for the benefit of their child's education.

Information on special needs

The class teacher is a key person to learn about the special needs of some children in the class. You will have met/will meet with the SENCO/Inclusion manager and been given targets and individual plans for some children. The class teacher should be able to help you to understand how these targets and plans are translated into everyday teaching and the specific needs of each child. It is important to know about any additional help or intervention groups children may have attended. If, for example, a child is in an intervention group, how can you make links between what is being taught in the intervention group and your teaching in the classroom? Discuss the best way of liaising with those leading the intervention groups. Also find out the strengths of these children so that you can boost their self-esteem straight away when they start in your class. Note that the lesson ideas presented in this chapter are easily accessible to all learners, which is important so that this first encounter with you is not stressful.

Ask the current class teacher which children are likely to find the change of moving to a new class difficult. You can help some children by labelling photographs of:

- yourself;
- where they will line up on the first morning;
- where they will hang their coat up;
- where they will put their lunch box.

The meeting with the current class teacher is important in collecting information about unsettling or traumatic circumstances that children may be encountering. These circumstances may result in certain behaviours which you should be aware of. If anything is of a concern to you, do speak to your mentor about how to approach any situation.

Data

You should have end of year class data that you should be able to discuss with the class teacher. Data should be available on:

- age;
- EAL;
- ethnicity;
- SEND;
- attainment and progress;
- any disadvantaged children who may be eligible for free school meals (FSM) and grants to decrease the attainment gap.

The type of data on attainment and progress will vary depending on the age of the children. At this stage, you need to be aware of the general needs of the class. Try very hard not to put labels on children and to immediately group them in terms of attainment. Instead, think of the challenge of every child reaching for the stars in your class with no limits on expectations. Data can be useful as it can alert us, it can raise questions about our practice, but it can also narrow our view of what we think children are capable of.

Routines/class set up

It would be really useful to understand the routines that the class teacher uses. Try to observe the class with their current teacher so that you can understand and potentially mirror some of the routines that work particularly well. Ask or observe how:

- children start and end the school day (handing out/collecting homework, lunch boxes, coats, bags, etc.);
- the children come into the classroom;
- the children settle once in the classroom;
- the children sit if they are on the carpet and who they are next to;
- the class monitor system is organised;
- upsets at playtime are dealt with;
- children are dismissed at different points during the day;
- how reading books are changed;
- PE equipment and changing is organised.

It often takes quite a long time to get a whole new system of routines underway with a new class, so taking on board routines that work particularly well already should make the transition between classes easier, so long as you feel comfortable with these routines. Carrying over some routines is also a way of making the children feel secure as there are fewer new things to get used to all in one go. Learning about the start and end of day routines will inform you about pupils' expectations so, if you change things, you can refer to what happened last year before explaining what will happen this year.

> *Draw on the excellent practice that already exists in the school.*

A complete set of books

Ask the teacher of the year group your new class will be entering into if you can have a complete set of books from 3 children. If children usually take books home at the end of a year, this may have to be explained to parents/carers but with an understanding that the children whose books have been chosen will receive them a year later. These books may be a really useful resource in understanding how learning is recorded and the level of challenge that is expected, as well as how some children may have received more structure to support their learning. Take some time to look at the progress from the beginning of the academic year to the end of the academic year.

Summary

Imagine the children coming into their new classroom in September with the class rules already displayed on the wall at the front of the classroom or the visual reminder of their class being a community of learners. The care and effort that will have gone into that display will be apparent and you will be able to use the display to remind the children of what you have agreed. This period of transition is about looking backwards in terms of understanding the children you will be teaching but it is also about looking forward and accepting the challenge of the possibilities of what could be. To get the best out of every learner you need to know them as individuals and as learners and to make them feel that they are part of a community where everyone is valued. Exciting times!

Check list

	Tick
I have:	
◦ met with the class teacher and found out as much as I can about the children I will be teaching;	
◦ learnt about the routines that the children use in their current class;	
◦ taken photographs of the layout of the children's current classroom as well as the classroom layout and displays of the year group they will be entering into;	
◦ asked if I can have a complete set of books from 3 children in the year group I will be teaching in.	
In the first lesson with my future class I have thought carefully about:	
◦ transitions in and out of the classroom as well as within the lesson;	
◦ how the content of the lesson can build up expectations of being in a new class;	
◦ how the material from the first lesson can be displayed.	
I know about the children's concerns about being in a new year group and have tried to alleviate their concerns.	

CHAPTER

8

The classroom as an empty box
Where do I start?

This chapter should help you to:

- have ideas for setting up your classroom;
- think about how the environment can help the special needs of some children;
- organise learning materials.

Introduction

Imagine walking into an empty classroom in the summer holidays with furniture stacked in a corner, no backing paper on the walls, and a messy stock cupboard. The decision-making as to where everything goes will be largely up to you. This chapter will help you to think about the decisions you have to make and to justify your choices with the particular needs of your class in mind. This chapter should provide you with some key principles to help you get started. You will need to fine tune this information to suit the age and learning needs of the children in your class.

Ideas for setting up your classroom

Clearing and labelling

Although it is time consuming, it is worth getting absolutely everything out of cupboards and drawers and seeing what is already in the classroom. You will then be able to throw out anything that you know will not be of use, such as used pens and out of date materials. If you are at all unsure about whether you should throw something out, do ask someone first. You can then start to organise the equipment and resources you have left. Some things may even need a good wash. Being organised with cupboards, boxes, and trays that are clearly labelled will save you so much time throughout the year. There may also be a shared area for resources for the year group which will need to be organised as a year team. It would be really useful for you to have an understanding of all the available resources in this area, so do spend some time looking through them and becoming familiar with the space. There will be some pieces of equipment that you will need to personalise, such as a wall stapler, as you will be lost without it if you misplace it.

The display boards will need to be cleared of any old staples. If you try to cut corners by putting up backing paper over old staples, they will just rip the paper, so prepare all the boards thoroughly.

Take ownership of the space.

Organising furniture

Hopefully you will have taken photographs of the last classroom the children were in as well as the classroom in the year group the children will be entering into. These will give you some ideas for classroom layout. It is always useful to try to incorporate some of the ideas from the previous year group. For example, if children coming from a Reception class are used to entering the class in the morning and choosing an activity for the first 15 minutes, this could be continued for the first few weeks in Year 1. If children are used to coming into Year 4 and starting the morning with a maths challenge, think about continuing this in Year 5. Some of these choices may require thinking about the position of certain pieces of furniture. For example, in my last Year 1 class when the children entered into the classroom the individual whiteboards and pens were laid out in a horse shoe shape with a phonics challenge on a standing whiteboard. This required a certain amount of space and equipment.

Think about where you will be standing for the majority of the time when you address the class. Now place the tables and chairs so that every child can see you easily. Look at the space around the tables and chairs. Can children access and leave their space with the least disruption to others? Sit in the chairs and make sure that as a learner you would be able to see the whiteboard where key teaching would take place, without having to move your chair or look awkwardly over your shoulder.

Some tables have inbuilt trays but in other classrooms the trays might be in a stand-alone piece of furniture. If you put the children's trays all in 1 area of the room you will have to be careful to only send a few children to their trays at a time. Placing trays near to where certain children are seated is probably easier. Again, sit yourself in some seats and check the journey:

- into the room to the table;
- from table to tray;
- from table to the carpet area.

Now think about where you can put well labelled resources that are accessible to the children. You should be trying to create a classroom ethos whereby the children become independent learners. If, for example, they need to use a number line, they should know where the maths equipment is kept and easily retrieve anything they need. Key pieces of equipment that are used on a daily basis should be stored on the tables.

Most classes in a primary school have a carpeted area for the whole class and where groups of children can receive focused support/input. Think also about the shape of the space: will all the children be able to see you and anything you want to show them easily? If you are teaching a group of children, will you still be able to see the rest of the class?

If you are lucky enough to have the space and available tables, set up an area for focus group teaching. Specially shaped curved tables can be found in some schools but if these are unavailable, 3 tables in a horse shoe shape will suffice.

Reading area

The reading area needs to be enticing whatever the age of the children. Try to create a particular theme, such as:

- cosy, with scatter cushions;
- cool, with pictures and quotes about reading from famous people;
- characters from the book the class will be reading;
- an enclosed space, with a material ceiling.

I have even set up outdoor tents in the summer term which the children absolutely loved reading in. It is always worthwhile going into bookshops to see whether they are willing to give you any cut out book characters or posters that are ex-display or even to have a look at how some book shops make their children's section enticing. I have also added suitable newspapers, comics, instruction manuals, pamphlets, even old annuals from my youth into the book corner; anything appropriate and of interest to get children reading. If you have the technology, do allow children to read books electronically and this may entice some children to read. Children also love listening to audio books. Do make sure that the material you provide reflects diverse culture and ethnicity. A multicultural classroom should be embedded with the choices we make as teachers, both in resources, visual cues, and learning materials that we use across the curriculum. The reading material and choices teachers make should also reflect the different make-up of families that children may encounter (in line with the school's relationship and sex education (RSE) policy). Spend time on creating this area of the classroom to entice all children to read as well as making them feel welcome and included.

First display space when you enter the classroom—the information board

The first display board when you enter the classroom can be an important area for key information. Class rules could be displayed here, as well as key information on every child in the form of a 'passport'. These can be displayed for your benefit but also for the benefit of other teachers that will be teaching your class.

Lion Class Passport:

This passport belongs to: Billy Richards	Passport photograph
What are your favourite subjects? My favourite subjects are writing stories and singing.	What helps you learn? If I am stuck, I am allowed to ask a friend for help. Rosa is good at explaining things to me.
How can teachers help you learn? Teachers can help me learn by not making me sit on the carpet for too long.	Anything else of importance I am asthmatic so I need to take my inhaler out to PE.
What are your greatest strengths? I am a good friend.	What would you like to be when you grow up? When I grow up, I want to be a pop star.

Also on this information board you can put:

- the weekly timetable;
- class rules;
- the list of jobs and names of monitors.

An information board will help you and other teachers.

The display space at the front of the classroom

Usually an interactive whiteboard and a board to write on is at the front of the class. The space around these boards should be used for key learning information. This is the direction the children should be facing when they are seated at their tables and so placing key learning information here is more useful than neatly backed art work. Try not to over crowd this area of the classroom with enormous amounts of information, but make the information relevant and helpful for learning. The following bullet points are all things that you should be drawing upon when you are teaching and children are learning.

The transition phase

Useful things to include are:

- the learning intention and success criteria (the success criteria may change or be added to);
- examples of learning in progress (this is sometimes called a working wall);
- a number line (I have always found having a number line running underneath the board really useful so that the children can actually physically use it);
- key vocabulary and possibly related pictures (using word cards for the key vocabulary can be brought into this space for each lesson and then moved to another point in the classroom until the next lesson. Always have spare cards so that you can add to the vocabulary in the lesson as sometimes you may have forgotten to include a key word or the children make a relevant suggestion);
- class rules (especially in the first few weeks so that they can be referred to regularly);
- visual timetable.

Regardless of whether you have children with special needs in your class, having a visual timetable is useful as it provides a clear structure for the day. If you have some children who especially need a visual timetable make sure you go through it at the beginning of the day and highlight when a lesson has finished. Visual timetables can be developed to allow children to get used to being a little unsure about what might be happening in lessons. The very basic timetables that follow show the progression from:

- **knowing** the lessons of the day;
- knowing that they **might** have PE or rehearsals;
- being completely **unsure** what might be happening after English.

Visual timetable:

Mathematics	English	PE	Computing

Visual timetable providing an alternative:

Mathematics	English	PE or rehearsals for Christmas play	Computing

Visual timetable providing some uncertainty:

| Mathematics | English | ? | Computing |

The visual timetable should be referred to at the beginning of the day and at the start of each lesson. Some children will like to cross off when a lesson is finished.

The remainder of the display boards

The classroom is a learning environment and therefore any display boards that are at the children's height should be used as a learning resource. For a Year 6 class, I would have key information that can be added to throughout the year. If the boards are then constantly used as learning prompts, the children should be able to visualise the boards and draw on the learning prompts when taking any tests. For example, in the past when Year 6 have been about to take a test in the hall, I would ask them to close their eyes and visualise the English display which had been referred to and used when teaching. Recently in a Year 1 class I observed a teacher taking a child over to a display that visually represented different numbers. The child was able to use the display to solve a maths problem. These are the best sorts of displays to have.

Display boards do not have to be instant; they can develop over time. For example, a topic board can start off with a visual representation of what the children know about a certain topic or even a question. The board then develops, depicting the children's learning journey.

One key thing to avoid with displays is children's writing that is beautifully backed, then put too high on a display board for any child to read. My belief is that most writing should have an audience, so stories and poems, for example, should sometimes be put in a reading area for others to read.

Art work and indeed representation of learning from all areas of the curriculum has a right to be celebrated and displayed. Displays higher up on a wall should be things that can be appreciated at that height.

Sometimes children come into school with information of somewhere they have been to at the weekend or a picture that they have drawn at the weekend. With some classes I have taught I have set up a display board where the children can post this information once they have shown it to me. This can develop the home/school link and an appreciation of the wider lives of the children we teach. A friend of mine taught a child who was fascinated by the discovery of Richard III being found underneath a car park. The child was profoundly dyslexic and hated reading but brought in the newspaper article he had been reading to share. My friend decided this was so important that she created a news and information board that lunchtime, pinned his article to it, and encouraged the class to add to it over time. Aside from having a huge benefit to pupils' awareness of important news, you can imagine the impact on that boy's self-esteem and perception of himself as a learner.

The learning environment and special needs

A special needs advisor walked into my first classroom and was brutally honest about the space as a learning environment. She told me the children were being bombarded with colour and there was an overload of information; in fact, the first thing she said was "*Whoa!*" She was right: it was like an Aladdin's cave, with things hanging from the ceiling wherever you walked and there was not one little space for anything else to be crammed onto the walls. I thought it was wonderful!

In my case, I was trying to entice what had been labelled a 'challenging class' into learning and yet, somewhere along the way, with my enthusiasm, I lost sight of creating an environment that helps children to learn. As I write this book, I realise that I cannot concentrate if there are patterns on walls. I like a simple, quiet environment to work in. The more you learn about 'special pedagogies' for children with specific needs, the more you begin to understand that many of the pedagogical approaches have the potential to help all children (and adults) to learn. Here are considerations when setting up a classroom; you will then need further adaptations for the special needs of individual children.

Special needs check list

Does your classroom have:	Tick
■ a visual timetable of the day at the front of the class;	
■ a predictable physical environment, e.g. the maths equipment by the maths display;	
■ clear labels throughout the classroom (words and photographs);	
■ a quiet zone with a table to work at where colours are soft and headphones can be worn;	
■ a computer that is screened off;	
■ organisers for table tops with markers for placement of equipment;	
■ an unfussy area at the front of the class that provides learning information;	
■ instructions (e.g. class rules) that are short and simple;	
■ backing paper for display boards that is softer in colour for at least 2 walls;	
■ specific equipment for some children?	

It can be seen that all these adaptations have the potential to benefit all learners. A quiet zone, for example, can be an area that all children are able to access and it should be viewed as a privilege to go in this area as opposed to an area that only some children are allowed to access. Children that need an environment with softer colours on the walls should spend the majority of their time facing these walls so be careful where they are seated. If you think you will be using a carpet area every day, the area behind you should be unfussy with soft colouring. There may be specific equipment for some children, for example, specially designed cushions to sit on or a wedged writing board. This equipment must be ready now for the first day of term for ease of transition for these children.

If you will be teaching a child who is easily distracted, they should be seated at the front of the class so that they will not have to look at the backs of children's heads. Other children should ideally not have to pass by their seat to get to equipment or trays and their own tray should be close by. If the child needs to give you an agreed cue that they need some time out, you are more likely to be at the front of the class to receive the cue.

As you are setting up your classroom, think about whether you need to have the lights on or blinds up, down, or half open. Be aware of the environment and sense which feels the most relaxed. Some children may be very sensitive to light or to the noise of the strip lighting in the classroom. You need to be highly sensitive to how the environment may affect some children. If you will be using a carpet area, make sure the children are not going to be distracted by corridor traffic or bright sunlight from windows.

Predictability is important for all children but especially important for some so do spend time setting up your classroom or learning zone carefully, as some children will find an environment that changes difficult to adjust to. It will be inevitable that you will need to make some changes over time. However, if you know that you have a child in your class who will find this particularly difficult, make sure you prepare them for any changes.

Organising learning materials

Books, pens, and pencils

Sorting the pens, pencils, and books needs to happen at this transition point. The checklist in Chapter 7 asks you to collect 3 sets of books of children in the year group you will be teaching in. This will give you a clear idea of the types of books required. You will need to check with your year leader or mentor if you can go into the stock cupboard and get all the appropriate resources. Do not do this without checking first, as books are chosen carefully for the appropriate age of the children. Some teachers of younger children like them to start writing on plain paper, for example, whilst others like the children to write on lines. There are many different layouts in books so to begin with, go with what has always been used and over time you should be able to make different suggestions if necessary. There may even be different books for different children in the class, depending on their needs. Similarly, with pencils, there are different size grips.

Pens, pencils, rulers, rubbers, and coloured pencils are usually kept on a central tidy unit on a table. These will become the responsibility of the children on the table. A mistake I made as an early career teacher was to allow children to use our brand-new electric pencil sharpener. This may seem a trivial thing to write about, but the disruption it caused with just about every child really needing to sharpen their blunt pencils was incredible. Also, I think we must have got through a year's supply of pencils in a term! I found a pencil monitor to be really useful, making sure that pencils were ready to use for the day ahead.

If they are appropriate for the children you will be teaching, little flip charts for tables are really useful. These can have A4 learning prompts in plastic wallets in landscape that can be added to for different subjects. These are really useful as some children will find it much easier to focus on learning prompts that are on their table as opposed to continually having to look up to the board.

Reading books

Get to know how the home/school systems with reading books works. The children and parents/carers will be expecting to have books and home/school diaries in the first few days of term. This will demonstrate that you are organised and following on from where the last term ended. If most of the children in your class are on a reading scheme, you will need to be familiar with the scheme and have all the books organised ready for the new term. The year group leader or English subject leader should help you with this. In your meeting with the previous class teacher you should have learnt how he/she managed to hear children read and change all the books. The new year group leader may have a different system but if you are asked by parents/carers of the changes at least you will be informed.

Summary

Setting up a classroom takes a lot of time but it is enjoyable, as you are taking ownership of the space in which you will be teaching. If you take time and effort to set your classroom up well, the children will notice the lovely learning environment that they will be entering into. Do not be afraid to be a magpie: walk around the school and take ideas from others and incorporate them into your classroom. Once you have set up your classroom, you will feel more settled, as you will begin to imagine yourself in the space. I would suggest having the classroom set up a good week before the term starts as this will give you some time to have a rest and prepare your planning in a more relaxed frame of mind.

Check list

I have:	Tick
○ organised and labelled resources;	
○ placed the tables and chairs so that all children can see me when I am at the front of the class;	
○ set up an information board just inside the classroom;	
○ created a reading area;	
○ found out about reading schemes, how readers are heard, and books changed;	
○ set up the area at the front of the classroom for key learning prompts;	
○ checked the special needs check list;	
○ collected and organised all the learning materials (books, pencils, etc.);	
○ prepared books.	

CHAPTER 9

Planning

This chapter should help you to:

- understand the key school policies and school priorities and the impact on teaching and learning;
- prepare for planning in the first half term;
- plan using school resources and routines;
- plan for the first week of teaching.

Introduction

When you were in your final placement school, the planning mainly consisted of the teaching and learning of the children in the class in which you were placed. This chapter makes you aware of the wider aspects of planning that are required in a school setting. The chapter also explores the planning required across a term, with a focus on preparation for teaching and learning and key events which, with careful thought before the term starts, should help you to pace yourself.

School policies and school priorities

When you were on your final placement, you were able to build up your teaching gradually. With your first class, you will be teaching for the majority of the time from the beginning of term. This is where you have to get yourself into the right mind set, as it is very unlikely that you will be brilliant at teaching every aspect of the curriculum straight away, even if you achieved the absolute top grade on your final placement. You need to be kind to yourself and realistic with an understanding that you will be learning throughout the whole of your career. In a way, this is what makes teaching so special as you never stop learning. All subjects are important and you will be teaching most subjects in the curriculum. Whilst I am a complete advocate of the importance of all the subjects in the curriculum, you need to focus on your Maths and English teaching first, as these are the subjects you will be teaching the most and the subjects that will be most important in terms of demonstrating pupil progress.

Read the policies and find out whether there are particular ways in which Maths and English are taught in the school. Recently, I was in a school where there was a focus in all Maths lessons on justifying answers and, in another school I visited, the focus was on Maths Mastery. In each school, the trainee teachers had to quickly adapt to the expectations of the school. This is the sort of information that is important to know. If a school has undergone a change in the way in which a subject is taught, the staff are likely to have undertaken specific training. You will need to get hold of key information that will help you to understand the approaches used.

If you are teaching Physical Education, for example, there may be particular elements of the policy that you must follow, for example, the way changing for PE is organised may be written into the policy for the higher year groups. An ICT policy may state whether you are allowed to use YouTube clips when teaching or whether or not you must view them in their entirety on the day you want to use them. It will be useful for you to go through the policies and highlight key things that you know you must adhere to and address right at the beginning of term.

There will certainly be a policy for planning trips and this will take some organisation. Do not let this deter you from taking children on outings as they have the potential to be incredibly rich learning experiences. If you know you are going on a particular trip, visit the place in the holidays after having read the policy. You will go with a different eye looking for:

- coach drop off and pick up points;
- the use of public transport;
- toilets;
- meeting points;
- a place to have lunch;
- information for helpers;
- how to organise the learning;
- accessibility for all children.

All newly qualified teachers should be supported in undertaking a risk assessment that is required for trips. Before organising day trips, try out smaller local trips that children can walk to, for example, undertaking a survey of the local shops. This will build up your confidence and highlight some key things that you will need to think about. Aspects such as the adult to child ratio or the way in which you organise getting a class across a pelican crossing all require consideration.

Planning for the first half term

In Chapter 6 it was suggested you get an overview of the term from your year leader or mentor. You now need to focus on the first half term.

The transition phase

Year 3 Half Term Overview

Maths	See scheme.	**Additional notes** Homework sketching parents/carers (frame and sell at Xmas fair). Parent/carer help required for cooking (dishes from different regions/ethnicities). Check health and safety and allergies.
English	■ Creating stories to read to Year 1 ■ Follow schemes for reading comprehension, spelling, and grammar	
Science	Forces and magnets	
Art and Design	■ Sketch books observations of people ■ Andy Warhol and Leonardo da Vinci studies	
Computing	Using search technologies effectively	
Design and Technology	Design and cook a variety of predominately savoury dishes	
Geography	■ Local study of human and physical geography ■ Compare with a region in a European country	
History	N/A this half term	
Language	Songs and rhymes in French	
Music	Composing own rhymes/songs (about Year 3 and being an individual)	
PE	■ Basketball ■ Gymnastics (partner work).	
PSHE/RSE	■ Friendship ■ Everyone is unique	

A half term overview will give you an idea of areas of the curriculum where you may have to undertake some research in order to feel prepared. This is worth doing at this stage so that you feel as confident as possible and not overwhelmed when undertaking your weekly planning sessions. Research on Andy Warhol, for example, may give you some ideas to contribute to the year group planning sessions. Looking at a half term plan in this simplistic form also allows you to see where there are possible links between subject areas. For example:

- PHSE/RSE can be linked to Art and Design with the children sketching each other and highlighting the uniqueness of each individual in the classroom;
- forces in Science can be linked to counterbalancing when creating a gymnastics sequence;
- spoken language in the English curriculum can be linked to the children creating stories that they will read to children in Year 1;

- in Science when timing toy cars moving down slopes of different surfaces, the children can present the results using their knowledge of graphs learnt previously in Maths;
- in Geography, the children can research their local area by using their understanding of effective search technologies learnt in their computing lessons.

Whilst each lesson will have clear learning intentions based on a particular subject, as a teacher you take opportunities to draw on learning from other areas of the curriculum. This helps children to learn by revising, consolidating, and applying knowledge and concepts already taught. For example, to actually 'feel' a force in a counter balance in PE helps a child to understand what might be considered an abstract concept. To write a story for a younger child and read it to them provides motivation and links 2 areas of the English curriculum together meaningfully.

Having an overview of the half term will also allow you to plan for the class of children to contribute to whole school events. Whilst on your final placement, you will have been very much focused on your particular class. Now you have to plan for involvement in the wider life of the school. The portraits in Art and Design, for example, would allow you to use something created in lessons at a Christmas Fayre in a very simple way. Self-portraits of the children can be framed cheaply and sold at the Christmas Fayre. Rather than being reactive to expectations during the term, try to plan for these opportunities now. This will be a real help to you in terms of pacing yourself and keeping on top of the work load.

Cooking a variety of savoury dishes in Design and Technology provides you with an opportunity to get parents and carers involved. There is also an opportunity here for dishes from different regional and ethnic backgrounds to be explored and linked to places being learnt about in Geography. Here is another example of how multi-cultural education is not an 'add on' but an integral part of decision-making during the planning stage. Always remember the health and safety required for any cooking and eating in your class: being aware of any allergies is absolutely key.

Make meaningful links between areas of the curriculum.

Class performances

Class assemblies do not need to be stressful and, if planned for in advance, can take advantage of the learning that naturally occurs in a half term. Taking the Year 3 half term overview, think of how you can draw on what will naturally be taking place in lessons to be used in the assembly. For example:

- performing French rhymes and singing French songs as people are coming into the hall;
- the theme of the assembly can be 'being unique' and what that means;
- each child says something that is unique about them (at this point, if you are in a religious school you can add some relevant material);
- include a section on the individuality of Andy Warhol and Leonardo de Vinci, highlighting 2 very unique and different artists;
- portraits of members of staff drawn by children in Art lessons can be projected on to a wall, or shown on an interactive whiteboard, and then the children and parents/carers can guess which picture belongs to which member of staff;
- finish the assembly by showing some drama undertaken in PHSE highlighting the importance of being an individual as well as a member of the class and school community (at this point, if you are in a religious school a prayer can be read);
- when everyone is being dismissed, the children can sing songs created in music lessons whilst sketches of themselves can be shown on the interactive whiteboard or projected onto a wall.

This example demonstrates how a class assembly does not have to be additional work and become stressful. Have as many group activities as possible, rather than getting individual children to learn lines. In this way, you will not become stressed if children are absent on the day: the children are also far less likely to become stressed if they are 'performing' in a group. Make sure every child contributes in some way. Also, if the assembly is created from their learning in class, the children should feel more confident in what they are presenting. There should also be minimal rehearsal time which is always positive.

Add music, movement, and group activities: think of variety.

The same approach can be undertaken with concerts. An approach I used with one Christmas concert resulted in:

- the set design for the production being undertaken in Art and Design lessons;
- costumes (tie dye) being made in Art and Design lessons;
- different light circuits made in Science lessons surrounded the name of the production in the entrance hall;
- advertising posters, tickets, and programmes written and designed by the children in English and Computing.

This approach will have to be adapted for the age range of the children you are teaching but the very youngest children at primary school can contribute to much more than just the actual production. This gives the children a sense of ownership and an understanding of 'real life' in terms of all the different roles that can be undertaken in the work of theatre. It also links learning together in a realistic and meaningful way. This approach needs to be planned in advance when you have an overview of the term and can start to see what ideas can be drawn from different areas of the curriculum.

Try to avoid rehearsals where children become stressed and bored by sitting doing nothing for long periods of time in the hall. This will make you stressed and it is a waste of time. Make the singing part of the music lessons where words are learnt through the enjoyment of singing with actions; avoid sending masses of lyrics home to be learnt. Take 15 minutes at the end of the school day in the classroom to 'rehearse' and, where possible, ask parents/carers to help at home. Aim to give everyone a part and, if possible, try not to give 1 or 2 children all the action. A week before the date of the concert, everything should be complete, the children should know what they are doing, and you should feel relaxed. You can then have 1 more rehearsal in the week leading up to the concert. This should be an enjoyable experience for all. It will be unlikely that you will have to lead a production in your first year of teaching but maybe you will and maybe this is your forte and something you will relish. If this is the case, make sure you have chosen the production during the summer holidays as it takes time finding something suitable as well as getting the performance licence.

> *Concerts should be a positive experience for all!*

After years of leading productions in school, I was invited to a Special school to watch their Christmas production. Three boys were meant to be performing a rap that they were really proud of. However, when the time came, they all froze on stage and made it clear that they really did not want to perform. The teacher just smiled at them and said, "*Don't worry!*" The concert continued but suddenly there was a shout of, "*We want to do it now!*" The teacher calmly smiled and said that it was not a problem. She found the backing music and allowed the children to perform their rap to enthusiastic and appreciative applause. I tell you this story because I think we have a lot to learn from it. Children can become incredibly nervous and performing can be quite stressful. I remember one of my own children calling out to me from the stage and the headteacher saying, "*Get him off quickly. He's going to ruin the show!*" He was 4 years old. The teacher I observed in the Special school was relaxed and calm and, most importantly, she put the needs of the children first. So, my message is to plan for any public performances in school and make them part of the learning process. Keep the needs of the children at the heart of whatever you are doing and in turn this will be a far more positive experience for all involved.

Resources and routines

The summer holidays are a good time to familiarise yourself with the resources around the school. You will have emptied out the cupboards in your classroom and become familiar with resources in Key Stage or year group areas. There may well be other resource cupboards for different areas of the curriculum. If this is the case, take some time exploring what resources are available.

Physical Education equipment

If you will be teaching PE, you will need to know how to get out the large apparatus in the hall. Ask someone to show you as it usually takes 2 people to pull out this equipment. It is crucial that you know how each piece of apparatus works so that you can check that the children have set up the equipment safely before they are allowed to get on it. Take photographs of where the equipment is usually stored in the hall as well as in the PE cupboard: this will help you to think about the organisation of getting out and putting away equipment correctly. If you are able to, create a board with pictures of the equipment on Velcro so that you can visually show the children where the equipment should be set up. Keep equipment in the same place for a half term with the same children getting out the same equipment. Think about routines such as:

- when the children enter the hall they sit like gymnasts next to the equipment they are responsible for and continue this routine for any transitions between equipment;
- using only the quietest of voices, they get the equipment out making sure they are always looking where they are going and walking around any equipment;
- you check the equipment;
- at the end of the lesson they put the equipment away and sit like gymnasts to show they are ready to go back to the classroom.

Check out the best places for you to stand so that you always have a good view of the whole class.

Routines like these will take time to embed but they will be worthwhile both in terms of safety and in terms of a calm atmosphere that in time will allow for greater time spent on the physical activity as opposed to losing time due to stopping and starting the lesson.

Outdoor PE

Check the outdoor space, in particular the line markings on the playground. Nearly all primary schools will have a netball court marked out. The curved section of the semi-circle of a court is a good place to get the class to stand, making sure they are not facing the sun. If the class can stand on the curve, you will be able to see every child. This is also a good place to model any demonstrations as every child will be able to see you. You can call this 'the base' so that when you say, "*Back to the base*", every child knows exactly where to go.

Next, look at all the available lines on the playground and think about how you might use the space. For example, a netball court has 3 equal sections; placing markers/cones down the length of the court creates 6 equal sections for children to play mini games. There are very many possibilities of how playground markings can be used.

> *When looking at teaching spaces think about how you can adapt them as well as creating routines.*

Information and communications technology

If you have a computer suite, check where is the best place to demonstrate and whether there is the facility to freeze the children's computer screens so they concentrate on your demonstration or instructions. Familiarise yourself with what the children are expected to learn in Computing and check the software and hardware available. Spend some time exploring learning opportunities and developing your confidence.

Now you need to explore what hardware and software is available to support learning in other areas of the curriculum, both in terms of what the children can access on computers in the classroom as well as what you can use to support learning on the interactive whiteboard. Do not get overwhelmed by all the available ICT available. In a year group planning meeting, you will undoubtedly be introduced to different programs as the term progresses. If you are in a single form entry school ask the ICT lead in the school to recommend key programs for your year group. I always found that it was useful to learn about and try something new every 2 weeks by asking the ICT lead to just spend 10 minutes with me rather than attending courses that I found a little overwhelming. When there is so much to take on board learning a little and often can be productive, especially when you are immediately putting what you are learning into your practice.

Planning for the first week of teaching

New teachers usually worry a lot about the first week of taking a new class; this is perfectly natural. You will probably find it useful if you over plan for the first week of teaching as this will help you to feel confident. You should plan just as you did on your final placement but make sure you have an open-ended question or challenge prepared at the end of lessons. You will then not be thinking 'on the spot' if the learning activities you planned are not challenging enough. Make sure that any planning takes into account the special needs of some children, ensuring that they can access all learning. Try to plan so that as much marking as possible can be undertaken in lessons and remember that there are different types of learning opportunities other than written. You should have time away from your class every week to plan and prepare. Make sure you know who is taking your class at this time and what they will be teaching.

During this week, make sure that you have a lesson on the class rules as well as a lesson on building the class as a community. Even if you addressed the class rules in your first meeting with the class before the summer holidays, you must return to them at the beginning of term.

Routines and knowing what is happening

Knowing routines in advance will allow you to feel calm and in control, both in front of staff and parents/carers. You will need to know how:

- children are collected in the morning and dismissed at the end of the day;
- children are sent to and collected from lunch;
- the register is filled in and any money/letters collected.

It is really important and useful to get the children into a routine for the first 10 minutes of every morning. In my Year 1 class, the whiteboards and pens were always set out on the carpet area in a semi-circle with a phonics challenge on the board; the children always sat in the same places so I knew learning partners could help each other if necessary. The children soon got into the routine of getting straight on with the challenge which gave me a chance to speak to any parents/carers if necessary. It also meant the children used the time well. In Year 5, different Mathematics challenges were on the main whiteboard, coloured according to difficulty. The children could choose whichever challenge they wanted. This was an excellent way to keep practising all the different Mathematical concepts that had been taught and again, I had the chance to speak to anyone if necessary. The class was set up the day before just in case something unexpected happened in the morning.

> *Meaningful routines can help children feel settled and ready for learning.*

If the children are new to staying for lunch or if they are having lunch in a different place for the first time, make sure that you accompany them to the lunch hall for the first few days to help them settle. Also be mindful of any children who may be new to the class; you may not be aware if you do not check. They would probably benefit from having a couple of buddies for the first week or so, to help them feel welcomed into the school. Also, at the end of the day, if the parents/carers are around, it would be really good to have a word with them, telling them how their child is settling into the life of the school. Always be mindful that only positive news should be passed on publicly. If there is something less positive, this should be in a classroom without the presence of other parents/carers. It is always better to have positive conversations whenever possible; these are easy to forget.

Sometimes having a routine at the beginning of the afternoon can also be really useful. In one of the classes I taught, the children would quietly start every afternoon reading with Baroque music playing quietly in the background. The regular timing of the music is meant to be soothing. The reading books were ready on the children's tables before they went for lunch which then minimised any fuss when coming into the classroom in the afternoon. This routine was especially relaxing after what had usually been an interesting lunchtime! A calm start to an afternoon can make all the difference to creating an atmosphere conducive to learning.

The routines and expectations you set up with the children will take time to establish so make sure in this first week you get the children lined up for key events like assemblies a few minutes earlier so that you can make sure they enter the hall quietly and calmly. Equally, at the end of the day, you do not want to be late dismissing the children so spend a little extra time getting the children ready. Giving yourself time to establish these routines will help, as you will be able to stop the children if your expectations are not being met without feeling flustered because of lack of time. Regardless of the age of the children you are teaching, they are responsible for tidying their classroom before going home at the end of the day. There may also be letters to be handed out; all these little things take time.

You need to establish routines for how dates and titles are written in books. How you want books to be collected and given out also requires consideration. A classroom can easily become a very muddled and untidy learning environment. I always found it useful to get the children to tidy up and get ready for the next lesson before going out to play or lunch. This promotes individual responsibility within a shared ownership of the learning space and resources right from the youngest learners.

If you have a class of younger children you may want to teach them the easiest way to get changed for PE, folding their clothes so that they do not get muddled as well as being easier to put back on at the end of the lesson. For older children, you may want to time them getting changed so that they can see if they can beat their time during the term. Choosing a piece of music for changing or for tidying up may be useful. These tactics will help ensure that more time will be spent on actively being engaged in learning as opposed to getting ready for learning.

Make sure any home/school links are well prepared this week, ensuring that you plan for the right reading books to be sent home and that routines are set up such as reading diaries and homework days. You will be likely to get some parents/carers wanting to see you this week so make sure you have a little time at the end of the day for a quick chat.

In all the years I spent teaching, I always found the first few days of term felt a little unnatural and my teaching was a bit stilted. I think this is very normal. It takes time to get into the flow of your teaching, as well as establishing class routines with a new group of children. Even as an experienced teacher, I never slept much the night before taking a new class. Would I still be able to teach? Again, this is natural, especially if the day before you had an INSET taken by an educational consultant introducing some new idea. Keep grounded, as you will not be the only person feeling a little daunted. As the week progresses and the flow of your lessons starts to develop and the children become used to being in their new class, things settle down and somehow the days fly by. Concentrate on the key things that will help you to be successful.

Do not be afraid to spend a few moments with the class engaging in relaxation exercises. Scrunching your shoulders up to your ears and then letting them completely relax: breathing in for 4 and out for 5. This will help you to relax as well as the children.

Remember to smile.

Summary

If you take a longer overview of planning and ask questions in advance if you are unsure, you are more likely to feel prepared and therefore secure in what you are teaching. This, in turn, should help you pace yourself throughout the term. What you want to avoid is becoming overwhelmed and reactive to situations. There will always be unforeseen events throughout a term, such as a teaching and learning governor observing throughout the school or a visit from a link inspector. If you are well planned and organised, you should be able to cope with these unforeseen events and take them in your stride.

You have now come to the time when you have done all you can in preparation for your new class and, if you have covered everything in this part of the book you will have done really well! Being prepared helps with your confidence and if you present confidently people will have confidence in you. Now you need to make sure you have a wonderful rest where you can switch off from school for a bit. Make sure the week before the term starts is free to catch up with your colleagues and to make sure your first weekly plan is ready.

Check list

I have:	Tick
∘ checked the school policies and highlighted key points;	
∘ an overview of the first half term's planning;	
∘ the resources needed for the first half term;	
∘ thought about how I can plan in advance in order to pace myself at busy points in the term;	
∘ looked at the spaces I will be teaching in and thought about routines.	

PART 3
The first year of teaching

The aim of Part 3 is to enable you to plan for the different aspects of school life that are likely to arise in the first year of teaching so that you are as prepared as possible.

Dear reader, you have made it to your first year of teaching! In all the years I have taught it is my first class that I remember the most. If I close my eyes I can see them now and remember their names. This is the class that had many teachers in the previous year, so I knew it was going to be a challenge. The first term was the hardest but I turned up every day and stayed as consistent as I could with rules that we had all agreed on clearly displayed on the wall. These were children with lots of energy so I knew I had to build movement into their learning and I knew I had to engage them. They needed to have a reason, a purpose for learning, so I tried as hard as I could to relate learning to 'real life'. "Why do we need to learn this Miss?" was something that was often asked in the first few weeks, so understanding the relevance of the learning needed to be explained at the beginning of each new topic.

As time went on, I gradually got to know the children and the children got to know me and they realised I wasn't going to leave them; I was staying for the year. They did test me that first term though: the boys' toilets were often flooded and graffiti was rife. On each of these occasions, I told them I was so disappointed, but never angry. They were testing me. I still stayed.

I soon realised that underneath the 'bravado' of some of the key characters there was actually a vulnerability. I needed to try to build their confidence. 'Fame' the music programme was very popular at the time and I used this to get the children singing, dancing, and writing scripts. The class made up their own version of 'Fame' which they showed to the school and parents/carers. They absolutely loved it, especially when they got to sing using microphones, just like the characters on the television. Their energy and apparent fearlessness needed to be harnessed in learning opportunities.

Instead of going to the Isle of Wight for the yearly residential trip, I begged the headteacher to let us go on an outdoor pursuits residential. This was one of the best things we did, as we really got to know each other over those few days. Children who were so confident in school were not necessarily the confident ones on the high wire! A really quiet boy saw that I was clearly not looking forward to going through the muddy, dark tunnels that were half filled with water. He told me to hold onto his boots and talked to me all the way through. I told him he was my hero!

I am telling you all of this because yes, teaching can be challenging at times. However, if you are passionate about getting all children to reach their full potential and keep trying to find solutions to help children to learn, it is so worth it.

It is no surprise that I start this part of the book on building relationships and community in the classroom. I have found that if you spend time learning about the individuals you teach and develop a sense of belonging and pride, learning will follow. We as teachers are educators and education is about helping to develop children to become part of a society who look after and value each other. This must start in the classroom.

CHAPTER

10

Building relationships and community in the classroom

This chapter should help you to:

- understand what a 'community of learners' might look like;
- understand different ways of building a sense of community with your class.

Introduction

For learning to occur, firm foundations need to be built so that children have a chance to reach their full potential. This chapter explores how these firm foundations might be built. It should help you to think about how to develop a community of learners where every individual member of the class feels a sense of belonging.

What might a 'community of learners' look like?

I am going to start this chapter in a very different way by telling you a story; a true story of a learning experience. In this story I am definitely 'the learner'.

I have always wanted to join a choir but was always wary of choosing the right one. Whilst some might label me 'musical' because I 'just about' play a couple of instruments, I am not the greatest singer, have some difficulties harmonising, but have always enjoyed singing. As a primary teacher, however, music was always a thread throughout the day: not a day would go by when you wouldn't hear singing coming from my classroom. Even as a university lecturer, I would include singing in some lectures.

My husband, Andrew, would class himself as not musical but he is someone who has always been an avid listener of music his whole life. He promised me that when we had a little more time on our hands, he would join a choir with me but, as the time got nearer, he was only promising to stay for a term. We didn't want a choir where we would have to audition, as we were sure we wouldn't get in! Also, Andrew doesn't read music, so that ruled out quite a few choirs. We wanted something vibrant but not cringy (I hope that makes sense). We put our names down for a couple of so-called community choirs, but in reality they seemed to be quite choosy and a little elite. Our eldest son, Tom, decided to try and help us look for a choir and thought he had found one that might suit us. We didn't research the choir but just put our faith in Tom and hoped that he had chosen well. We booked up for our taster session and turned up for the last rehearsal before Christmas; definitely not an ideal time to have 2 complete 'newbies', as they seem to be called in this choir, turning up on the doorstep. Andrew and I, 2 teachers with years of experience, walked into a new learning space where we felt trepidation! We popped our heads around the door, "Welcome to the computer course!" the man said. Oh no, we had come to the wrong place. He held our gaze for a couple of seconds and then broke into the biggest of grins. "Only joking! Come in! Come in! Why are you looking so scared?" We replied saying that we had never been in a choir before. "So? Come in!" he replied. "I'm Mark. What are you, a soprano or alto?"

"I haven't got a clue", I replied.

"Well, from the sound of your voice I think you might be an alto. Sit over there", he said with a deep voice indicating I must be an alto. Georgie, Yamini, Josefa, and Emma immediately welcomed me into the fold. Emma and Georgie creating a space for me between them, whilst Yamini and Josefa smiled so reassuringly. Andrew and I wanted to sit behind everyone and just listen but Mark insisted that we joined in.

Andrew went to sit with 2 other men in the tenors. I knew he would feel really vulnerable as he had never harmonised in his life. Would he even make it to week 2? Mark could see that Andrew was a little out of his depth and brought the tenors to the front where he could help support them. He put his arm around Andrew and helped guide him through some of the songs, recognising someone in need but not making a big fuss about it. Being placed between Emma and Georgie was an immense help to me as they clearly knew what they were doing and there were plenty of other singers in the alto section. Every now and again in their quiet ways, Emma and Georgie whispered reassurances.

During our first term we have come to realise that there are some significant features of this choir. A massive emphasis is put on everyone getting to know each other, especially names. Nearly every week, Mark asks us to find out something new about someone in the choir. He is not really interested in us talking about our jobs, but wants us to find out about each other as people. For instance, every week we find out what has happened in people's lives, someone's child might have been in hospital or we briefly discuss a great film someone has watched. We get to know one another and as a result we can be a support to each other. I have been quietly supported by a member of the group who has a different skill set to mine this last term; nothing to do with singing! Recently Karla, a really new member of the choir, has been raising money for African Vision in Malawi by cycling 500km with her parents. The support on WhatsApp from the choir felt as though everyone was physically supporting them . . . it was awesome. Ordinary people but an extraordinary group of people

So, we feel welcomed, we get to know each other and then we must learn to sing!

This is a choir where we are challenged. Mark certainly does not provide us with material to learn that is easily achievable. Instead, there is a clever balance of enticing us with his beautiful arrangements that draw us into wanting to learn with a level of difficulty *that seems a little out of our reach at first. The material is cleverly broken down into manageable chunks and gradually built up until we cannot imagine what we have actually achieved. We do not, however, get praise if praise is not due. "That was O.K.", Mark will say, lengthening the O and the K with a grin. We all know that means it really wasn't very good at all. However, we get praise when praise is due and so it is valued. We are even challenged, at times, to come to the front and sing and take risks even if we get it wrong; this is called the 'pressure cooker'. People are, however, always clapped for their efforts and an extra loud clap is given to someone who takes this risk for the first time. This can also be a great way to model to others how a piece should be sung. It also makes us self-evaluate and realise that different sections need more work.*

Time is taken to promote the ethos of the group, highlighting the need to be supportive of one another. Mark will model how it is useless if 2 people who know what they are doing exclude someone who needs help, albeit unintentionally. He models what we should be doing and, as a result, people are given clear instructions as to how an inclusive environment is created, which in turn raises the standards of all in the group. Imagine if all the great singers sat together and those who struggled sat in another group. We are a community of learners who help each other.

So here Andrew and I are, just about to start our second term. The WhatsApp group is vibrant with people sending messages saying how much they are looking forward to choir. Andrew has said the holiday has been too long as he needs to practise! I find myself trying to harmonise along to songs on the radio, sometimes successfully and sometimes definitely not! So what is it that creates this vibrant learning environment? It is the leader, Mark. He's in control (well most of the time!), he absolutely knows his stuff but also says that even he can get things wrong sometimes (although I haven't seen it yet), he values every individual, he challenges us, and he constantly promotes the values that he so clearly holds.

Thank you Mark De-Lisser.

You are the most inspirational teacher I have had or seen in my very long career in education.

This story tells us so much about building a community of learners, the benefits, and the ability of a teacher to create such an environment. Your challenge as new teachers with your first class is to have someone write something similar about the learning environment that you have the power to create for the children you teach. In terms of community, the story teaches us about:

- welcoming people;
- looking after each other;
- helping each other learn;
- belonging;
- learning from each other;
- what an inclusive environment might 'look like';

- valuing every individual;
- the importance of knowing learners as people.

In terms of teaching and learning the story teaches us about:

- modelling;
- chunking learning;
- having high expectations for all;
- motivation;
- appropriate humour;
- not putting a ceiling on expectations.

The following quote from a member of the choir also makes us think carefully about the importance of valuing the contributions of every member of a class.

Valuing every individual is something that I feel really strongly about. At choir, I feel valued for being me. I feel like I can be entirely myself which is so refreshing and real. Also not putting a ceiling on expectations really rings true with me. In so many situations in my life, I've had the 'wind knocked out of my sails' whilst doing something I love, because I am not as good as someone else, or will never be the best. At choir, I feel valued, I can achieve what I want to, and it doesn't matter how 'good' I am. We support and encourage each other.

Laura

This quotation demonstrates how this feeling of being valued is so important in a learning environment and how a teacher has the power to knock the confidence out of a learner so easily. I understand that we all need to develop resilience when learning but there is something so special about a teacher that also understands the fragility of learning, uses mistakes as a learning tool, and empowers learners. It may interest you to know that after 2 terms in the choir Laura is one of the most competent singers in the altos! In this learning environment she has flourished.

Different ways to build a sense of community with your class

Morning greetings and end of day routines

Ensure that you establish a routine at the beginning and end of the day when every child feels welcomed into the learning environment. Making eye contact is really important in making a connection. Picking up on certain clues when you look a child in the eye can maybe prompt you to have a quiet word with them and check whether they are feeling alright. Alternatively you might really surprise a child by saying "*Good morning*" to them in their home language.

These small but highly significant interactions enable a child to understand that you have taken the time and effort to engage with them on an individual level. Asking a question such as, *"How are you feeling today Jack?"* at the classroom door can be highly significant, acknowledging that a child has been off sick and asking after their well-being.

Routines and behaviour

Being part of a community means adhering to the rules and routines that have been understood and agreed by all members of the class. Chapter 7 in the second part of this book provided you with ideas on how to develop a shared understanding of the class and school rules. Now you need to establish these rules. Children generally like continuity, boundaries, and fairness. Establishing the rules and routines tends to make children feel secure and this in turn will help to develop a sense of belonging. Use inclusive language such as, *"In Year 5 class we agreed to listen when someone is speaking."*

Celebrating effort as well as achievement

In order to create an environment where everyone feels valued, ensure that children's efforts, determination, and resilience are rewarded as opposed to just achievement. Also for some children, really small but significant achievements should be rewarded. This has the potential to create a very different classroom ethos. In this way you can ensure that everyone has a chance of being rewarded and therefore everyone should feel more valued. This in turn should motivate children. Be careful though: rewards must be earned. If you over reward, it can become meaningless. Also do not forget that some children prefer a quiet word such as, *"Marika, I was so proud to see you speaking with such confidence in the class assembly today."* Not all children like to have their achievements shouted from the rooftops.

Celebrating different achievements

Ensure that you celebrate all different types of achievements. Make sure if a child has a particular skill in subjects such as Art or Dance, they are acknowledged. Also make sure skills, knowledge, and achievements outside the classroom are also celebrated, such as Tae Kwondo or a knowledge of trains, etc. Again, this should help children to feel valued for what makes them an individual and you as their teacher will begin to understand the 'whole child'.

Seating plan

Think carefully about how you are seating children. Be flexible according to what you are expecting the children to learn. If, for example, you are using discussion in an English lesson, it would be far more beneficial for some children to be interacting and learning from the rich language of more articulate children. Remember, children may exhibit a current level of ability because of what they have experienced so far in their lives, whereas they may have the potential to be highly articulate. Think about how you would feel if you were in the group that you knew was the 'lowest English group' (what a terrible term) and stayed in that group for most of your learning. Being in a community means having the chance to interact and learn with different children. So when it is appropriate, mix children up so that they can learn from each other. A friend of mine taught in a school where every Monday morning, from Reception up, they would draw named lolly sticks to create new talking partners for the week. This reinforced the sense of 'team' alongside the fact that each pupil was expected to work effectively and respectively with every other member of the class.

Having a voice

In your class who will get to:

- be the class representative on the school council;
- have the lead in the school play;
- show visitors around the school;
- answer the most questions in class?

These are just a few situations where teachers have the potential to demonstrate that they value the contributions of all children and sometimes put their faith in giving a child the chance to shine, like taking a lead in the school play. Rather than just having a quick vote for a class representative for the school council, for example, find out who has already been a representative, who would like to have a go, and who would really benefit from having additional responsibility. Have this discussion before any possible voting. Give different children opportunities to lead.

Understanding one another

Knowing the children in your class as people should be a key focus in the first term. Chapter 7 in the second part of this book provides some ideas of how you can begin to develop a sense of community with different and unique individuals making up a class. Having something visual to represent the community of the class is really helpful in creating a class identity or perhaps a class song that you can develop by adding different verses during the academic year.

With my first class, I created a medium term plan for the first term that explored 'emotions'. This enabled me to begin to understand the different needs of individual children. It also helped the children to understand themselves, as well as understand other members of the class. Images by Keith Haring are superb as a catalyst to start exploring emotions. The children in my class looked at different images and described what they saw in terms of emotions. They then chose music to match a particular emotion. The hall became a really enormous art room with very large pieces of paper and different coloured paints available. The children listened to the music that they attributed to emotions, mixed colours, and painted patterns and shapes that depicted an emotion. The children then used the painting and music to create dances. Throughout the term, intermingled with these lessons, the children explored their feelings, wrote poems, and expressed how they felt. This was a great way of beginning to understand the children as individuals.

We can do this ... we can show people what we are capable of!

Entering your class into a competition is a great way of getting your class working together. There are often borough competitions or even national competitions that you can enter. One of the classes I taught entered a borough competition about the importance of looking after the environment. The children researched, wrote poems which were turned into songs, created dances, and made their own costumes out of absolutely anything green. There was no sewing involved, just old clothes as a base onto which anything could be stuck or safety pinned.

There was enormous pride in the fact that the children had taken ownership of what actually went into their 10-minute song and dance performance, with a very clear message to the audience. I acted more as a facilitator. With my guidance they worked together ensuring that everyone had a chance to be at the front of the stage at some point. The sense of working together truly helped the community spirit within the classroom. Also the sense of 'being in something together', regardless of the outcome, was really special. They won the borough competition which was extra special.

Classes can work together on smaller scale projects such as being the most environmentally friendly class. These smaller scaled achievements can be something to be really proud of. Make sure the children hear the words, "*I am really proud to be a member of Year 1 as we have shown how we can work together to make a difference.*" Notice the language of inclusion here; you are positioning yourself as a learner and part of the team.

Looking after the environment of the classroom and each other

Some schools give each class a budget and usually the class teacher spends this on things the class needs. I got into the habit of explaining the class budget to the children and having a class discussion on what they thought we should spend the money on; usually scissors and glue sticks! The children would work out how many we needed and what the cost would be and the amount left in the class budget would be displayed on the wall with pictures of what we had bought.

Because the children were part of the decision-making, they developed a real sense of looking after their learning environment. Every glue stick was found and the tops put on with children berating others for not looking after the equipment properly. You do not necessarily need a budget for this to work: instead, you can start off the year with an inventory of the resources in the learning environment. Children can be given jobs looking after different things.

In order to develop a sense of belonging and respect in the community of the classroom, the environment should mirror the different ethnic and cultural backgrounds of the children, their family make-up (within the boundaries of the school's RSE policy), and the world beyond the walls of the classroom. Ensure resources (pictures, reading material, etc.) achieve this. Do not forget that parents and carers can also be a fantastic resource.

Have a discussion with the children about the different monitors that are needed to look after the class environment. Also discuss what would be a fair rota so that everyone plays a part in some of the less favourable jobs and all have a chance to undertake the popular jobs.

The children need to be encouraged to look after the environment and each other for the well-being of the whole class.

Get the foundations in place

It is really easy, especially as a new teacher, to concentrate on just teaching and learning but in order for learning to happen the foundations for learning must be built. Children definitely have a sense of the teacher that makes them feel safe, a class that they belong to, and a place in which they are respected for who they are. As learners they will then feel more able to take risks and have a go at things that are difficult. They will learn to support others around them and hopefully reach their full potential.

Education is also so much more than academic achievement. It is learning about being part of a society that values individuals that look after each other so that they may all achieve.

Summary

What is it about the teacher who has the X factor that makes children want to be a member of their class? I have thought about this so much in my career and have wished that I could capture all of the key ingredients and share them with others. We can learn the science and the craft of teaching but it is also an art with skills that are highly intuitive in understanding how to enable a class of children to be the very best group of individuals that they can possibly be. Sometimes it is the smallest things that are hard to quantify, such as a teacher winking at a child for getting through their spoken part in a play: the silent 'well done' of that wink can mean so much. In all the education books I have read, I cannot remember the word kindness being used as a key ingredient for being a teacher. You can be firm, consistent, and kind and the children can know that you are always thinking about what is in their best interest.

Check list

	Tick
I have:	
○ built a morning and afternoon routine to greet and say goodbye to the children;	
○ displayed the class rules that have been agreed by all members of the class;	
○ displayed a visual reminder of the class as a community (see Chapter 7 in Part 2 of this book for ideas);	
○ discussed the different jobs needed in the class and agreed on the rota;	
○ thought carefully about how children are rewarded.	
I try to make every child in my class feel valued and welcome.	

CHAPTER 11

Preparation and planning for the progress of children

This chapter should help you to:

- understand important elements of long term, weekly, and daily planning;
- understand how to plan for the progress of:
  - special needs
  - intervention groups
  - unexplained underachievers
  - disadvantaged children;
- understand equal opportunities for all children.

Introduction

This chapter will help you to think about the preparation and planning that is required throughout the year, term, weeks. and days. Up until this point, you will have mainly been involved in thinking about units or schemes of work, weekly planning, and daily planning, but now you need to have ownership of the complete diet of learning opportunities that the children receive. Also, you need to ensure that you are mindful that you will be responsible for understanding the learning needs and progress of all children, irrespective of whether they are in the classroom learning with you or if they are sometimes learning with someone else.

Long term planning

Long term planning is having the overview of the year which can then be broken down to outlines of what is to be taught in each half term. This should help to demonstrate that there is a balance of different subjects taught during the academic year and that there is progression in what is being taught. Sometimes, when looking at an overview of the year's planning, things can be moved around if there is a more logical link between different areas of the curriculum. When teaching Year 5, I moved the teaching of statistics and graphs to fit in with the teaching of Athletics in the Summer term. The children monitored their progress in Athletics and recorded their results in spread sheets on computers. This information was then put onto different graphs and aspects of statistics, such as finding the mean, median, and mode, were taught using 'real' data from their jumps, throws, and running times. If you know that you have a residential trip in the Spring term, it may be worthwhile linking a particular genre of writing, such as creating an advertisement for a trip to a seaside town or an information pamphlet for a visit to a nature reserve. Try to make learning 'real' and meaningful.

Highlight and revisit learning

Chapter 9 in Part 2 looked at how you can make links between subject areas so make sure these links are made apparent in your teaching. For example, if forces are being taught in Science you can link to Gymnastics by talking about the push and pulls in counter balancing, but you must highlight these links when teaching the children. Also be mindful of ensuring that you take opportunities to keep revising learning that you have already taught; trying to keep it 'alive' for the children. For example, when lining up, chant 3 spellings that the children keep getting wrong, or revisit a times table, or ask a question such as, "*What do the internal angles of a triangle add up to?*" The whole class replies in unison with a certain pitch, "*180*". You are now responsible for the progress of the children, so you need to take opportunities to revisit learning already undertaken and not let prior learning slip away. Remember, physical changes take place in the brain when learning occurs, so you need to make sure learning is refreshed so it can be more easily retrieved when necessary.

Weekly planning

Now that you have the overview and ownership (possibly joint ownership) of the weekly planning, you can potentially have a far greater input into the diet of learning opportunities that the children receive throughout the week and each day. Earlier in the book I referred to the 'light and shade' required in planning to ensure that children encounter different types of opportunities to learn. They can learn individually, with a partner, or in a group or maybe they can learn through drama or film. When planning you will also need to think about the energy levels of the children. Children are usually more tired in the afternoons, especially on a hot summer day. Also think about which subjects can be taught in succession, for example after an energetic Physical Education lesson the children are more likely to be responsive to a potentially 'quieter' learning environment such as Computing.

You need to think about your energy levels as well as thinking about subjects that you find more challenging to teach. If Science and Computing are 2 of your weaker subjects try not to teach them on the same day as you may find this stressful. On a Friday afternoon try to teach something that has the potential to be more peaceful and will not require marking, such as PHSE. Your energy levels will gradually decrease as the week progresses and so will the energy levels of the children. If you plan the week carefully you are more likely to harness the learning potential of the children. Try to spend the last 20 minutes at the end of the week getting the children to review their learning. Finally dismiss the children with a calm routine at the end of the week. You may want to shake every child's hand and they can tell you their biggest achievement that week: this takes a little time and children need to prepare for what they will say.

Daily planning

Even trainee teachers find it hard to sit and be passive learners for a 2-hour lecture (I am not advocating that this is a good way to lecture), and yet I often find fairly young children are sat listening for long periods of time. You need to plan for a variety of different learning opportunities in daily planning. If you are in a single form entry school you will have ownership of this planning. If you are in a year group, you will plan the week with the year group, but the ownership of how these plans are personalised for the children in your class is important. Within a morning or an afternoon, you need to think about a varied diet of learning opportunities. Children will need to have opportunities to:

- talk about their learning;
- learn with others;
- be quiet and contemplative;
- listen carefully (but not for too long);
- engage in different learning opportunities;
- move and be active;
- sit and concentrate.

Plan for different types of learning opportunities in a day.

How long you expect children to sit and be quiet will vary according to the age and individual needs of the children. If you think about planning for a variety of different learning opportunities you are less likely to have low level behaviour issues. If children spend most of the morning learning in near silence, it is quite natural for them to 'explode' at lunchtime.

How to plan for the progress of children with special needs

Revisit Chapter 4 in Part 1 to remind yourself of some key pedagogical approaches that benefit all children but in particular children with special needs. You will need to have read key reports for individual children and be honest about whether you fully understand the reports and ask for help if necessary; you may not have come across some of the terms used. The key question is what implications do these reports have for you in terms of planning for teaching and learning? For the majority of the time, if not all the time, children with special needs will be in the class being taught by you, so you need to be aware of the high quality and targeted provision each child requires.

Ask if you do not understand.

Know the targets for a child and know exactly what changes in learning you need to see over a specific time. For example, by half term Tom must be able to:

- read the first 20 key words in the reading scheme;
- write his full name;
- answer a question in a full sentence.

The outcomes for Tom are:

- **s**pecific;
- **m**easurable/meaningful;
- **a**chievable;
- **r**ealistic;
- **t**imebound.

Keep the key outcomes in your planning folder where you will look at them at weekly planning sessions so that they form an integral part of your weekly and daily planning. When you are lining up for assembly, you might ask all children to write their name in the air, but concentrate on Tom. You might start the day with 3 key words hidden somewhere in the classroom and Tom has to find them and tell you or a friend what they say. You might ask a teaching assistant to record Tom's answers in the plenary so you can collect evidence to assess whether he is answering in full sentences.

If Tom has some 1:1 teaching out of class, maybe with a SENCO/Inclusion manager or a speech therapist, you need to be mindful that you have an overview of what Tom is learning in these sessions (and possibly how it is being taught) and have feedback on his progress. You need to reinforce and possibly extend the learning taking place out of class in the class, where appropriate. You are the gate keeper of Tom's progress whatever provision he is receiving; this is a really important point to remember. Tom and his parents/carers must always be part of discussions, they must have a voice and be part of any decision-making. Approaching special needs as a team is key.

Tracking the progress of the outcomes of children with special needs is extremely important and for some children you need to make sure you celebrate small but significant steps in their learning. *"Wow! It's only week 2 of the term and you have learnt 5 key words already. Brilliant! Let's tell your Dad after school."*

Intervention groups

Intervention groups can have a different focus. It may be that some children need extra help in certain subjects, or for emotional and social well-being, behaviour, physiotherapy, or anything where there is a particular need for a group of children. You need to know the expected half termly outcomes for each child and have an overview of what is then being taught in sessions. If you have a child who finds it hard to manage anger, for example, it will be key for you to follow key strategies learnt and practised in the intervention group in a class situation and playground situation. If a child is having physiotherapy and finds it easier to sit on a large ball rather than on the floor, you can incorporate this into any carpet time in the class. Intervention groups can be short term so when appropriate, it is especially important for you to carry on with key strategies in a class situation.

Unexplained underachievers

You may analyse the progress data for your class at the beginning of the year or at any point during the year and realise there is a group of children who are underachieving. These children may not have special needs and do not necessarily require a specific intervention. This is when you will need to undertake some additional targeted teaching as part of everyday lessons. In Mathematics and English lessons, I always ensured that in the main section of the lesson I taught at least 1 focus group, usually 2, rather than wandering around a class trouble shooting. Your TA can have a focus group, but one which he/she can leave and be the trouble shooter. This allows you to spend uninterrupted time focusing on a group of children. All children should have focused teaching from you but you can ensure the group of unexplained underachievers receives an extra focused teaching session with you in the week. I found this a really useful way to target the teaching of specific children in order to ensure the expected progress of all children in the class.

Disadvantaged children

You may have children in your class who receive funding to help narrow the attainment gap between themselves and their classmates. Senior leadership should decide how this money is spent, as it will depend on the needs of the children. Sometimes 1:1 help can be given or groups may be set up if the needs are similar. These children may require an environment particularly rich in language, or there may be gaps in their learning. Whatever their need or whatever intervention is in place, it is the high quality daily teaching from you that will be a key factor in the child succeeding. Once again, if the child is out of the class for any time, you will need to have an overview of provision so that you can reinforce learning in the classroom. Keep a close eye on measurable progress.

Equal opportunities

'Equal opportunities' is an interesting term and it can often be misinterpreted as meaning that we should treat all children the same. Why should all children be treated the same if they are different? The intervention groups and special needs provision, for example, are there because some children need it. We are giving them an opportunity to succeed.

We have to be very careful as teachers when we use terms such as 'very able' or 'lower ability'. You only have to go online to look at the school reports of some famous people to see how some teachers have completely missed something very special and promising about their pupils and given them a most inaccurate label. Some children may not have had the same opportunities as others, so you need to make sure that these children have as much chance of succeeding as possible. Be wary about putting a ceiling on the expectations of children. Be flexible within a lesson; if a child is finding something easy, ensure that you challenge them, alter your expectations. If some children are struggling, stop and create a new focus group. Be flexible in approach to meet different needs. If a child has limited spoken language, you need to give them as much opportunity as possible to engage with others in a language rich environment. They will not thrive if they are seated with other children who have limited language.

Think about what opportunities you are giving all children to demonstrate what they are capable of. At the planning stage, what opportunities are you giving children to demonstrate how creative and inventive they can be? During lessons, are you allowing children to question and debate? I remember a child coming up to the front of the class and taking the pen out of my hand to demonstrate an easier way of tackling a Mathematics problem. Sometimes when I tell people this, they gasp, as if this was a terrible thing for the child to do. I think it was great that the child thought they could do this. The child was right. He did have a more succinct way of finding a solution to the problem and I thanked him. He went on to study Mathematics at Oxford University. Allowing children to reach their full potential is also about classroom ethos and giving children time and space to demonstrate what they are capable of as well as developing an understanding that a classroom is a team of people at different stages of learning.

Every child in your class has the right to have you, the professional, teach them. So, in the main section of lessons during a week, every child should have a focused group teaching session with you; this includes children with special needs.

Summary

After a few years of teaching, I taught a child with Down's Syndrome in my Year 5 class. I was particularly worried about how I was going to teach forces. I had always ensured that my teaching of the concept was practical but I thought it needed to be far more practical for the learning needs of this one child. As I was thinking, I looked outside the classroom and saw the local playground which was situated right next to the classroom. It was like a light bulb moment. Why had I not thought about using the playground as a stimulus and learning resource for all the children? Centrifugal force could actually be felt on the roundabout and gravity felt on the slide! I really began to think about planning in all subjects more carefully. For example, in Geography we were going to be learning about the water cycle, so Dance that term became all about the journey of a rain drop. I learnt a lesson that year; I had become complacent in my planning and this one delightful child had awakened my love of teaching and learning. It taught me that making learning practical, memorable, and making meaningful cross curricular links helps all children to learn.

Check list

	Tick
I have:	
◦ planned for meaningful cross curricular links and highlight these when teaching;	
◦ planned for different learning opportunities across the week and during each day;	
◦ planned so that all groups of children are taught by me.	
I am:	
◦ able to embed the outcomes/targets of children with special needs and children in intervention groups in weekly and daily planning;	
◦ able to be flexible within lessons in order to meet the learning needs of children.	

CHAPTER 12

Language and learning

This chapter should help you to:

- develop the language of learning and the environment for learning;
- develop the 'golden thread' of learning throughout a lesson:
  - the quality of modelling
  - understand the key elements of focus group teaching
  - understand the importance of the plenary for learning
  - the language of feedback for learning;
- the language of behaviour for learning.

Introduction

I believe the language of 'learning' should be at the heart of every classroom and the word 'work' banned. A bold statement I know! This then has the potential of creating a learning environment where the children understand their role in the process of learning as well as taking shared ownership in their own development. This chapter explores how to make this a key feature of your practice and classroom ethos. The chapter also highlights key elements of teaching that should help you to ensure that high quality teaching is taking place so that the children have the best chance of making progress. There are many different approaches to teaching but if you master the key elements set out in this chapter, you will have built a firm foundation from which to further develop your pedagogical skills.

Developing the language learning and the environment for learning

The classroom 'space' can become known as the:

- Learning Zone;
- Learning Pod;
- Learning Space;

- Learning Hub;
- Thinking Space;
- Learning Bubble;
- Brain Control Centre;
- Centre for Learning.

Your class can help choose the name that depicts the space as somewhere where they will learn. This may seem really obvious and we know that learning takes place all around us, and not just in the classroom, but sometimes children view the classroom as somewhere that they have to work as opposed to learn. You have to be really focused in ensuring the language that you use is the language of learning.

Make the focus on learning and not on working.

The language of work	The language of learning
"When you have finished your work you can go to lunch."	"You can go to lunch when you can show me what you have learnt."

If a child goes to lunch knowing that they have mastered some learning, they have demonstrated self-improvement; they know that they will have benefitted. Completing work can seem more like meeting the expectations of the teacher.

Focusing on the language of learning as opposed to work does not mean that children will not be working hard in your class. It just changes the emphasis to them as a learner instead of you being the enforcer of the completion of work. Children need to understand that in order to learn they must:

- persevere;
- rise to the challenge;
- understand strategies they can use when they find things hard;
- know how to improve on their learning;
- understand how they learn best;
- understand the feeling when they finally achieve something they could not do before!

Use stories, animated short films, and inspirational clips of real people who have struggled in order to achieve. Make a fictional character or real person a focus every half term and use them as inspiration. Select stories and clips carefully so that you can explore the emotions and skills that are linked to persevering and rising to the challenge of succeeding. Refer to these emotions and skills when you are teaching and when children are finding something hard. They will then recognise that frustration, perseverance, and resilience are all part of the learning process.

Finding learning a struggle is important and every child should experience struggle as part of learning. Earlier in the book I mentioned a child in class who was amazing at Maths. I remember reflecting on whether I ever truly challenged him as he always got everything right. This became my goal. The reaction of the child when he was stuck on a Maths challenge for the first time was amazing; he just could not cope and was so angry and frustrated. My mantra to him for the rest of the year was, "*Good. If you are stuck you must be learning!*"

Another way I got children to persevere with their learning in Maths, for example, was to put the solutions to algorithms they had been given around the classroom. However, there were a couple of answers that were incorrect. The children had to work together to find the correct solutions. Imagine a teacher putting out incorrect answers! They learnt that they needed to be resilient, that I might try and trip them up, and that they would have to work out the answers for themselves.

It's good to be 'stuck'.

As a learner, you cannot struggle all the time so there must be periods of time when children are given opportunities to enjoy the knowledge, skills, and understanding that they have gained. Imagine the challenge of learning to sing a difficult harmony to a song, finally mastering it, singing it with the other parts, hearing the beautiful harmonies together, and then being asked to learn another difficult song straight away. Learning must be consolidated and enjoyed, so make sure you give the children these opportunities.

Equally, when someone has achieved something that they have been aiming for, make sure you really celebrate. Be careful, as for some children you will need to make sure you celebrate much smaller steps in learning as they will be significant to the child. I remember one headteacher, when she was particularly pleased with the progress of a group or class of children, lead a celebratory dance around the school making as much noise as possible! It was a sight to behold and those children really knew that they had achieved something special.

Make some noise!

Independent learners

As teachers we need to teach children how to become independent learners. Chapter 8 in Part 2 of this book is devoted to thinking about how you might set up your classroom for learning. If you have thought logically about putting the clearly labelled Maths equipment under the Maths display, for example, children will automatically know where to go to get equipment to help them with their learning. You might want to organise learning partners so that they can ask each other for help. For most of the time, a quiet learning atmosphere where children can ask each other for help or move in order to get the learning equipment they need is an environment that is conducive to learning.

Think of the stages the children need to go through before they come to you for help:

- Stop! Take time to work out how to do something by yourself first;
- look on the working wall to see if there are any learning prompts;
- get some equipment that might help;
- ask your learning partner;
- ask an adult.

Teach the children to become independent.

How much do you talk and how much do you allow the children to talk?

It is my belief that the quality of 'teacher talk' is one of the most important factors in a classroom. However, it is really easy to talk without checking that the children are understanding, by using words that children might not understand, such as; 'the mouth of a river', 'the source of the River Nile', 'the embankment'. Check by asking what the meaning is, rather than saying, "*Do you understand?*"

Think about the quality and quantity of your language when teaching.
Do I:

- give the children only the information they need?
- chunk my language (give information in small, precise chunks)?
- check children's understanding of key words?
- allow all children to talk about their learning?

Be brave and record yourself for 5 minutes only. Self-reflect on:

- how much surplus language you use;
- the quality of your questioning;
- how much time you speak and how much time the children speak.

Remember, when the children are speaking, you are assessing their learning. If you continue to speak, you have no idea whether they are learning or not. Children can be so motivated and absolutely bursting to talk about their learning, so if only 1 or 2 children are allowed to answer questions this can be quite disappointing for the other children. Allowing partner talk not only allows the children to clarify their thinking and potentially extend their understanding, it also allows them the opportunity to be far more engaged in their learning.

With partner talk, make sure you get involved so that you can gauge the children's understanding.

Be brave and ask children how you could have explained something better. This is a powerful way to demonstrate to children that you are prepared to reflect and take on board advice. You will also get an honest answer!

Are you talking too much?

Let the children talk more about their learning.

Develop the 'golden thread' of learning throughout a lesson

The golden thread of a lesson is what you are expecting children to learn. The golden thread should be apparent in the learning opportunities you provide for the children. Too often in planning the thought is, "*What do I want the children to do?*" as opposed to, "*What do I want the children to learn?*" and sometimes the golden thread of learning is lost.

There are different ways of presenting the golden thread of learning at the beginning of a lesson:

- learning question;
- learning objective;
- aim of the lesson;
- learning intention;
- we are learning about;
- what am I going to learn?

Whatever term is used the children need to be clear about what they are trying to learn, so make sure it is always in language that the children understand and that it is achievable. 'Today we are learning about the time', is too broad, so be really specific. When you are specific, you can accurately assess whether learning has taken place.

'Can I use adjectives to describe a character in my story?' is the golden thread that is made apparent at each stage of the lesson in the following example.

Introduction	Can I use adjectives to describe a character in my story?
Mini plenary 1	Underline the adjectives you have used so far to describe your character. Look at Nadika's description (under the visualiser) and help me underline the adjectives. What other adjectives would help us know what he looks like?
Mini plenary 2	Read the description of your character to your learning partner. Make a suggestion of an adjective that would make the description of the character even better.
Plenary	What have we been learning about? Have we used adjectives to describe a character in our story? Let's listen to some examples of writing and see if the adjectives help us draw the character being described. What other adjectives would help us with our drawings?

Use the language of the golden thread throughout a lesson.

The quality of modelling

The quality of your modelling is so important—the precise language you use as well as clear visuals and prompts. Do not just model and assume the children will understand; work through an example, getting the children to actively participate. Ask key questions to ascertain the level of the children's understanding and get children to justify their answers.

How do you know? Why do you think that?

If you find that most children in the class need your help in the more independent learning stage of the lesson, you need to return to the modelling stage and break down the learning further. Be adaptable and flexible and react to the needs of the learners.

Using modelling in mini plenaries can be a really effective way to refocus the children on their learning. Using examples from the children at this stage can be really effective: "*Let's put Nadika's writing under the visualiser and see how she has used adjectives to describe her character.*" Modelling can also be used in the plenary to demonstrate how a child's writing could be improved even more with a little help from the rest of the class.

Focus group teaching

Focus group teaching is not about sitting at a table monitoring a group of 6 children tackle their individual work sheets. Focus group teaching should be the teacher engaging with a group of children to assess their level of understanding and to develop their understanding. Through discussion with the children, you might draft the first 2 sentences of an opening paragraph to a story, taking their ideas and extending the quality of the sentences with thoughtful questioning.

You may have 6 children who need more teaching on long division, so you undertake some focused group teaching. All the time you are teaching and questioning individuals in order to gauge their level of understanding. Gradually, they should need less of your input.

The quality of your interactions and questions in group teaching should enable you to really understand the learning needs of the children you teach. Ensure that every child in a class has focused teaching with you. This is crucial for you to truly understand the progress of all learners in your care.

The importance of the plenary for learning

The plenary is a key assessment point in finding out what the children have learnt or whether there are misconceptions or difficulties in understanding. The learning objective, learning question, or whatever term you use should be returned to as well as any success criteria. It may be appropriate to return to 'modelling' and questioning to ascertain exactly what or where the children are experiencing difficulties in their understanding. What you find out about the children's learning should inform the planning for the next lesson.

The plenary is also a great time to 'hook' the children onto the next stage of learning. Pose a question, a problem, or a puzzle that will make them go away and think and look forward to the next lesson.

What were we trying to learn? Have we learnt it?

The quality of your questioning will enable you to know the depth of the children's understanding.

Example 1

"What shape is this?"
"It's a cube."
"Well done Ben."

The child may know the 3D shape is a cube or he may have guessed.

Example 2

"What shape is this?"
"It's a cube."
"How do you know?"
"Because it has 6 faces, each face is a square and they are the same size."
"Ben, you have really learnt about cubes today. Well done."

The child definitely knows the 3D shape is a cube.

Using real life learning opportunities

Try to highlight to children how learning can be useful to them: "*We are learning about report writing as some of you might become a journalist when you are older, for sport, local news or even for pop concerts.*"

You are giving children the opportunity to explore and develop a skill that may be of use to them. The teacher that entices children to learn and gives meaning to learning is far more likely to see better progress and behaviour because the children are motivated: "*We are going to create a museum of World War II for Year 4. You will be their guides and will need to write a pamphlet for them to take away.*"

Writing stories or poems that are never read is a real shame, so always try to get the children to read to an audience. The children are then becoming real authors. Year 4 may even write stories for Year 1 children and ask what characters they would like in their story. Children partnering younger children and hearing them read on a fairly regular basis puts the children in the role of teacher. It is a great skill to develop in children: understanding how to prompt a reader, asking meaningful questions, and developing the skill of inference: all benefit from this process.

The language of feedback for learning

Marking

Giving feedback to children and allowing time to respond to feedback is part of the process of learning. There is absolutely no point in taking books home to mark and then not giving the children opportunities to respond to your marking. If you have marked books and highlighted how children's learning can be improved, time must be allocated to respond to the marking. Some schools use the term 'polishing pens', whereby children respond to feedback to improve their learning. Other names can be used such as 'reflect and improve time'. Whatever it is called ensure it becomes routine and helps to make sure the marking is directly related to what the children are learning. The very best marking is that which is done with the children, when they receive feedback in the lesson and can respond immediately.

Children giving feedback to each other

Make sure children are given opportunities to help each other improve. This will not happen automatically; children will need to be taught how to do this. It is too easy to say, "*Look at your learning partner's writing and give 2 stars and a wish*". You will need to model how this is done. Children need to give feedback explicitly on the success criteria. Initially they find it very hard to actually give 2 stars and a wish, so you may need to build up to this. Once this becomes a regular part of lessons, partner work is a great way for children to assess and develop their learning. Talking about their learning is part of the learning process. When a piece of writing is read aloud, children can hear mistakes or when a child explains how to use a protractor to a learning partner, their own understanding becomes clearer.

Allow children to give feedback to each other.

Self-assess

Having check lists for children to self-assess is useful.

I think I have:	My partner thinks I have:	My teacher thinks I have:	
			■ labelled the X and Y axis;
			■ plotted the 4 co-ordinates to make a regular shape;
			■ created my own regular shape on the same graph and recorded the co-ordinates.

It is easy for children to tick that they have completed something but it is always useful for this to be followed by sharing their self-assessment with a partner.

There are other methods of finding out children's understanding, such as thumbs up or down, colour coding, smiley faces, etc. In order for these to work you need to develop a classroom ethos in which children can be absolutely honest. The classroom ethos cannot be underestimated. These systems only work if action is then taken if children are communicating to you that they are finding something hard. If a number of children put their thumbs down mid lesson in a mini plenary, what are you going to do about it? This is when you need to be adaptable and flexible in order to meet their learning needs. The progress of the learners in your care should be at the very heart of your teaching.

Be flexible and adapt to the needs of the learners.

What have we learnt this week?

Make sure you make time at the end of the week for children to reflect on what they have learnt. You might remind the children of the key learning opportunities in the week and get them to discuss with their learning partner what they think they have achieved. The children might even have a 'learning journal' where they reflect on what they have learnt, using pictures, diagrams, or words.

- What are they proud of?
- What was really challenging?
- What do they need to improve to be a better learner?
- What have they learnt this week?

If you use a fictional or real person as inspiration to understand about the process of learning, you can refer to them at the end of the week in a class discussion. This should help to develop a shared understanding of learning. With Year 6, Michael Jordan may be the inspirational person who is the focus for the half term. You could discuss the following quote: 'First learn to fail. I've failed over and over and over again in my life and that is why I succeed.'

Talk about what this means and the different feelings he must have had when learning to play basketball at such a high level.

As the children leave the classroom on a Friday afternoon, get them to tell you one key thing they have learnt that week.

The language of behaviour for learning

Inappropriate behaviour is often the result of:

- learning opportunities that do not meet the learning needs of the children;
- missing key steps in the learning process (e.g. after discussion, missing the critical stage of how to transform thoughts into a piece of prose);
- too much or too little time allocated to a learning task;
- learning opportunities that do not motivate or engage children;

- children not understanding the point of learning;
- children not understanding the skills required for learning;
- not feeling part of a learning environment.

We all have lessons that do not go so well and if we are really honest and reflect on why this might be the case, it is often something that we could have done better in the planning or delivery stages of the lesson. There are, however, always going to be children in your class who will challenge you and you have to be prepared to use language that will defuse situations and help find solutions. It is very easy to be reactive (especially when you are tired) and so you need to have key strategies to help you where the use of language is key.

!	The language of choice
"Jack you know you can't bring footballs in class. Put it in the cupboard now." "No. I want to keep it here." "If you don't do as I ask you will have to stay in at breaktime." "I don't care." "Put it in the cupboard now." "No."	"Jack I see you have a football under your desk." "Yeah." "The school rule is no footballs in class Jack. You can either put the football in your PE bag or in the cupboard until the end of the day. The choice is yours."

!	The language of rules
"Sabrina no running in the corridor." "But Mr. James just saw me and he didn't tell me off." "Are you answering me back? I think you need to see me at break time."	"Sabrina no running in the corridor." "But Mr. James just saw me and he didn't tell me off." "What's the school rule about walking in the corridor?" "Yeah I know." "Remember the school rules are there to keep us all safe. I've reminded you of the rule so make sure you walk in future."

!	The language of praise and direction
"Sir, sir, please can I answer this question?" "Marvin, you are always shouting out. I am absolutely fed up with it!"	"Sir, sir, please can I answer this question?" "Marvin, when you can put your hand up quietly, I will ask you." 2 minutes later "Well done Marvin, you put your hand up quietly. Now you can answer."

!	Name the behaviour and not the child
"Isobel you are a really naughty child!"	"Isobel, drawing on the wall was not the right thing to do. What do you think you should do to make things right?"

!	The language of direction
"I want to play with the Lego." "No. You have to finish your writing."	"I want to play with the Lego." "First you must finish your writing to show me you understand and then you can play with the Lego."

The alternative approaches to managing the situations allow children to take ownership of their behaviour and to hopefully make the right decision, learning from their behaviour. There is also more of a chance that you and the child are going to build a more positive relationship where learning is more likely to occur. There will be times when you feel incredibly frustrated, and this is when you must try to think from your head and not your heart, but do not be too hard on yourself when you do make mistakes. I remember telling a child who had misbehaved that he would have to miss playtimes for the rest of the week! What a ridiculous statement. This reaction was more about my frustration. What the child needed more than anything was to run around and let off steam. I should have carefully followed the school's behaviour policy and taken time to think about what I was saying, as opposed to reacting to the behaviour the child presented.

Summary

Teaching can be broken down into some key elements that have been presented in this chapter. In reality, addressing all these elements consistently is challenging. The key is to keep self-reflecting and being honest about whether you are truly addressing all the elements in the check list. Also praise yourself when you know you have done well. Sometimes focusing more on one element of teaching, for example, your questioning, is a good way to improve.

A way to ensure your classroom is an environment focused on learning, as opposed to completing work, is to ask the children 'what' they are learning and 'why'. This will give you a clear insight into the clarity of the learning thread in the lesson. One of the beauties of teaching is knowing when what you have taught has made a real difference to the learner.

Check list

	Tick
I teach children about the process of learning;	
I am able to:	
◦ chunk information	
◦ get children to justify their answers	
◦ probe answers;	
I provide plenty of opportunities for children to engage in talk when learning;	
I model learning opportunities and gauge children's understanding whilst modelling;	
I keep the 'golden thread' of learning at the heart of my teaching;	
I provide opportunities for children to improve their learning;	
I use language that helps children to own their behaviour and to be ready for learning;	
I can adapt and be flexible in order to meet the learning needs of the children.	

CHAPTER 13

Building professional relationships

This chapter should help you to:

- understand how to develop professional relationships with:
  - parents/carers
  - teaching assistants and learning support
  - your headteacher
  - your mentor
  - office staff, lunchtime supervisors, cleaners, and site manager.

Introduction

Being a teacher in a school is multi-layered in terms of your role. The significance and importance of the different relationships that you engage with cannot be underestimated. This chapter will help you to think carefully about these relationships. Relationships within a school environment are key to creating a harmonious professional environment. It would be very easy to skip this chapter and think it has less significance than some of the others, but in my experience these relationships are crucial and you will have your part to play in becoming a valued member of the school community.

Parents/carers

The terminology of parents/carers means those adults who are the primary carers of a child; for example, for some children this may be foster parents or grandparents who are bringing up their grandchild. For this chapter, the term parents will be used with an understanding that this term encompasses all primary carers.

Primary teachers are really significant people in a child's life. There is an enormous amount of trust that is required to hand your child over to someone else for a large part of the day. Therefore, the relationship between parents and their child's teacher is so important. Clear communication, careful choice of words, and understanding the perspective of the parent will help to build trusting, professional relationships.

Beginning and end of the day exchanges

Engaging with parents is one of the biggest differences when you have your own class. The amount of time you engage with parents will depend very much on the age of the children that you teach; with younger children you are likely to see parents on a more regular basis, if they are taking their children to and picking them up from school. It is important that this transition at the beginning and end of the day is smooth. Chapter 9 on planning highlighted the importance of setting a routine at the beginning of the day so that the children can come into the classroom and engage in a learning task straight away. This then gives you an opportunity to have the occasional 2-minute chat with a parent. In this time, you may be given some important information that will allow the parent to feel settled for the rest of the day, knowing that you have listened to their concerns. The child may also feel more settled and you may have information that will help you to understand the behaviour of the child. It may be that you will have to arrange another time to meet if more time is required, but you can reassure the parent that this will be arranged as soon as possible. It is these small but significant exchanges that will help to build up a positive relationship with parents.

Always try to ensure that the majority of beginning and end of day exchanges are as positive as possible, making sure you engage with all parents over a period of time and not just those who are perhaps easier to talk to or those that demand more of your time. Occasionally there will be a parent who takes up an unacceptable amount of your time. You will need to nip this in the bud early on. A useful way is to state at the beginning of the conversation that you only have 2 minutes so the conversation is timebound.

In your new class, there may be 1 or 2 children who presented with more challenging behaviour the previous academic year. The parents may have been called into school to talk about their child's behaviour on a regular basis. Catch these children being good as soon as you can so that the first interaction with the parent is positive, telling them what a great day their child has had in school, maybe showing the parent (with the child) an imaginative picture they painted, some great story writing, or about their beautiful singing in Music. Highlighting the positive is so important, both for your relationship with the child and the relationship you will need to build with the parent. This will then help if you need to talk with the parent about their child's behaviour at any point.

With a child higher up the school, for example in Year 6, where you might not see the parent, ask your mentor if you can phone the parent up to tell them something positive that has happened. This is nearly always a shock to a parent whose interactions with teachers is not usually positive. Again, this is a good way to start to develop a relationship with the parent. Friday after school is usually a good time to phone; great news for the child and the family at the start of the weekend.

Talking to a parent about their child's behaviour

It is never a good idea to ask a parent at the end of the day to come in and talk about the inappropriate behaviour of their child in front of all the other parents. The parent will feel as though they are being told off and feel embarrassed. Be discreet; any conversation is for you and the parent of the child concerned, not for the ears of the other parents.

Always label the behaviour and not the child as naughty when talking to the parent. I think it is nearly always a good idea to have the child present with the parent to talk together about how you can help the child to make better choices. Hopefully the child will then see you and the parent working together as a team, ultimately wanting the best for him/her. Try also to explain the things the child does well so the parent hears something positive. Arrange a time when you will talk again when you will both feedback to each other, so as a team you are monitoring the progress of the child.

Tricky situations

People usually present in certain ways for a reason. If you were someone who had struggled in school you may feel pretty anxious about your child having to go through what you went through. If you were bullied you may react quickly and angrily if a child was unkind to your child. If you were someone who was under enormous pressure to succeed academically you may inadvertently put similar pressure on your child. There are many reasons why parents react as they do but it is part of our job as teachers to build professional relationships with all parents.

If a parent is agitated, upset, or angry and wants to see you, ask the parent to sit down with you. If you feel unsure about meeting the parent on your own, arrange to meet them the following day. You can ask your mentor or a senior member of staff for advice in the meantime. Sitting down as opposed to standing with an agitated or angry parent can usually help to defuse a situation. Listen to the parent's concerns without interrupting. Try to find a solution to the problem together and make a date and time to review progress if necessary. If appropriate, give reassurances that you will do whatever you can to help or monitor the situation in the meantime. For example, if the parent says the child has no one to play with at lunchtime, you must reassure them that you will ask the lunchtime supervisors to check on their child as well as asking the lunchtime supervisors for feedback. You could ask other children to make sure the child has company. If you have time, you could check on the child or ask the senior member of staff on lunchtime duty to check. You must then feed back to the parent. You will usually find the parent presents in a very different way because someone has listened and acted on their concerns.

Please note that if you are ever presented with unacceptable behaviour from a parent, you should stop a meeting and say it will need to be rescheduled with a senior member of staff.

Try to finish a tricky conversation with a handshake.

Suggested format:

- sit down together;
- listen without interrupting;
- try to find out a solution together;
- give reassurances where you can and seek advice and help;
- thank them for coming in and sharing their concerns;
- feed back to the parent at a later date.

Try not to be defensive if the parent is cross because of something that you have done, such as kept their child behind at playtime. As with nearly all situations it is the language you use that can ignite or defuse a situation.

!	Diffusing the situation
"Mr. Jones I am really cross you kept Kai in at lunchtime." "Well Mrs. Hughes, he hadn't finished his work and I told him it needed to be completed before lunchtime."	"Mr. Jones I am really cross you kept Kai in at lunchtime." "Well Kai didn't make the progress expected in the lesson and I want him to make the progress I know he's capable of. I'll always make sure he gets plenty of time outside at lunchtime. That 10 minutes extra made all the difference to his learning."

Parent consultations

Parent consultations may be called different names and may be run in very different ways. Whatever they are called, the key discussion is about the progress of the child. Make sure you prepare well for these meetings, with all marking up to date. Your mentor will help you to prepare but usually it is good to make sure you have information on:

- key progress data;
- evidence of what the child has achieved;

- key targets for progression;
- how the parent(s) can help.

Stand up and shake hands (if culturally acceptable) with the parent(s) and welcome them. If this is the first parent consultation of the year, the parents will want to know how well their child is settling in. Try to think of giving information like a sandwich:

- start with the positive;
- relay any key information for improvement here;
- finish with the positive.

Be honest about any key information required for improvement but choose your words carefully and make sure it does not sound as though you are telling the parents off for their child's behaviour or lack of progress. If you know you have something you are worried about saying, bring it up in your mentor meeting and ask for advice. Practise what you are going to say.

!	Careful choice of language
"Megan can't sit and concentrate for long."	"Megan needs to move often and this helps her learning. I'm thinking of giving her a squidgy ball as I think this might help her to concentrate."
"Zac hardly ever puts his hand up and shouts out most of the time."	"Zac is beginning to put his hand up in class instead of shouting out, so this is something I am going to concentrate on."
"Alka still needs to be in the intervention group for phonics."	"Alka is benefitting from being in the intervention group for phonics."
"Chelsea still gets angry sometimes in the playground."	"Chelsea is beginning to control herself when she feels angry; so she's making some progress."

Finish the consultation by standing up and thanking the parents and state that you are looking forward to seeing them again. Be careful as it is really easy to go over time. It is not always easy to start a consultation when parents have been waiting for a long time.

Keep to time allocation at parent consultations.

Demonstrate that you value all children

Children and parents in particular will know whether their child has, for example, had 'star of the week'. Some parents will be waiting week after week to see whether their child has been made 'the star'. Your record keeping for these types of awards are absolutely key. I remember a parent telling me that their child was nearly always the last to get star of the week in every class he had been in. So, we need to be aware of how these outward facing awards might impact on the child as well as the parent, who can become anxious for their child. Think also about making sure that every child has a chance to speak and take an equal part in the class assembly. Parents will usually make every effort to make these types of events so make it worth their while. For productions, do the same children have the lead parts or are you encouraging others to have a go? Engage parents to help their child cope with a challenge of taking on a lead role for the first time.

Building professional relationships with parents can be really useful in helping a child to reach their full potential. Sometimes, some difficult discussions are required, for example, if a child requires different provision for their special educational need that their current school does not provide. As teachers, we cannot underestimate how some parents must feel at times. You will develop your understanding of engaging in these different situations but at every stage of your career there should always be people there to help you.

Teaching assistants and learning support

Teaching assistants (TA)

If you have a teaching assistant, this is the person you will be working closely with on a daily basis. You will need to know the strengths of your TA so that you can build up their confidence in working with you. Imagine being a TA who struggles with Science and the new teacher happens to be a Science graduate and in the first lesson they are given a work sheet on forces for their group of children during the lesson. You must plan ahead and pre-empt this type of situation from happening so that your TA is well prepared for the lesson.

TAs will vary in their experience, so you need to be flexible in your approach. If, for example, they are relatively inexperienced you may find it easier to give more guidance. If you have an experienced, effective, and established TA, acknowledge this and make sure you take time to reflect on how well the partnership is developing. It can be quite daunting having an experienced TA who has taught in the school for a number of years. It will require tact to make any changes. Go slowly and use inclusive language.

!	Inclusive language
"Maureen, I've decided to change how we do fruit time this week."	"Maureen, I thought we might try organising fruit time like this. Let's have a go this week and see how we get on."

You are the lead professional in the classroom and you are responsible for day to day decision-making but including your TA in some changes should help to develop positive professional relationships. There are some key points that should be noted regardless of the experience of your TA.

Make sure your TA:

- knows what they are teaching in advance (ask if they need time to check anything over with you);
- is given instructions on how much and what type of support to give (you might need to model this);
- is not just put with children with special needs (these children have a right to be taught by you);
- is engaged in partner talk, mini plenaries, and the plenary.

In time you should be able to deploy your TA according to the learning needs of the children in every part of the lesson. For example, if you find in the introduction to a lesson on fractions some children clearly understand the concept being revised, the TA can extend the learning of these children by taking them as a group whilst you continue teaching the rest of the class.

I have worked with many TAs, one who was absolutely exceptional. I am ashamed to say that it was a while before I realised she had a French degree and 'A' Level Mathematics. Probably a term was wasted in the ineffective deployment of this very able individual. She was someone who could turn her hand to anything and she was never flustered if I decided to change things mid-way through a lesson. As time progressed, she came up with ideas of her own and she always asked if she could try something new out. There was mutual respect and we both understood our roles.

I have also worked with someone who was very new to this type of work and needed far more guidance. I would make sure that my instructions were really explicit and provide appropriate sentence starters at times or guidance on how to hear readers, for example. This all has to be managed very carefully with phrases such as, "*I found this really helpful when I started to hear readers. Have a look and let me know if it's helpful for you too.*" Sometimes you may have to model how you would like things to be done or how much guidance you want your TA to give the children. Understanding the level of help you give to children is quite a skill; it is your job to ensure your TA understands your expectations.

Learning support assistants (LSAs)

LSAs are usually employed to support one child. This can be quite intense for the child if the LSA is constantly next to the child. Also, it is quite an art to know when you can gradually withdraw the level of support so that the child learns to become a more independent learner. As the class teacher, you need to be involved in these dynamics; this can be achieved by ensuring you also plan and review with the LSA in the same way that you would with your TA. Make sure a child who has an LSA also has time being taught by you. It is only when you teach the child that you will be able to begin to fully understand their needs and have meaningful conversations about the provision for the child with the LSA and SENCO/Inclusion manager.

All children are entitled to be taught by you.

LSAs will also come with different expertise and experience. It may be that the LSA has supported the child over a few years and knows the child's history and particular needs really well. You will need to research the particular needs of the child so that you can engage in the level of discussion required with the LSA.

Positive relationships with TAs and LSAs are built up over time. The support staff that I have spoken to have all said that what they need is clear guidance. A teacher who is worried about leading creates uncertainty whilst a teacher who provides clear guidance provides structure. Do not be afraid to be open and honest when you have given your TA/LSA some guidance and it had not really worked. I always believe it is never an issue (no matter how experienced you are) to say, "*I got it wrong. Sorry*". I think a great deal of respect can be earned from being open and reflective about your own mistakes.

Model the importance of saying thank you and please at all times and make sure the children value the support they are given by any additional staff.

Demonstrate how much you value your support staff.

Headteacher

The interactions with your headteacher will definitely be more than when you were on your final placement as a student teacher. The interview panel, of which the headteacher was almost certainly a part, have put their faith in you and should be extremely interested in looking after your well-being; they have invested in you.

Headteachers are always observing their staff around the school with regards to the interactions with colleagues, children, support staff, parents, office staff, and visitors. They will probably pop into lessons occasionally and will learn a great deal from these informal visits. Acknowledge the presence of the headteacher when they come into your class and perhaps get a child to show some excellent learning or something they are really proud of. The headteacher will sense your confidence and feel confident in you.

The headteacher will expect you to have a voice in staff meetings, so do not be afraid to speak up as well as making sure that you listen carefully and take note of the experienced voice of others. Demonstrate that you are absorbed in every meeting and never take your phone in so that you will not be tempted to look at it.

Part 1 of this book mentions the need to caution about volunteering for too much on the final placement. I think the same advice can be given to any newly qualified teacher. There is a real balance between wanting to please everyone and volunteering for too much, so be careful as you will have enough to do with managing your own class of children but do show willingness to help out when necessary and show that you are able to be part of a team. Ensure you take time to say, "*Good morning*" and "*Have a lovely weekend*" and all the necessary pleasantries that make a working environment more pleasant to work in. All these things get noticed and help to build up positive relationships. The well-being and harmony of the staff should be important to a headteacher. Demonstrating that you are a team player and 'fit in' with the rest of the staff is essential.

The headteacher is your assessor, usually along with others in senior leadership. The key message I have got from headteachers for newly qualified teachers is to understand the importance of being able to take on board advice and to not confuse advice with criticism. You are in a profession in which you will be forever learning. Trainee teachers may have completed their final placement with an excellent grade, but this does not necessarily transfer into the first year of teaching. The expectations of being responsible for your own class is so different from the comfort of having your class teacher ultimately in charge and responsible on final placement. My biggest piece of advice for developing a positive relationship with your headteacher is to always demonstrate that you are open to learning. Soak up their advice and ask for further help if necessary. Going on a course may help your teaching of Mathematics but there is nothing like observing excellent practice in your own school or asking if someone can come and teach alongside you, or observe you. Even if this can be achieved for just the introductory section of a lesson, you will have had some feedback that is context related. I think this is invaluable for your own development. Be proactive and ask for this support if it is necessary. Do go and speak to the headteacher if you have any major concerns that you think they need to know about.

It is usually the headteacher who you will meet to talk through the progress of the children in your class. Be prepared for these meetings by talking through key points with your mentor and the SENCO/Inclusion manager beforehand. Data is important but is very easy, at times, to allow teaching to be narrowed down to just data. Children are individuals and things happen that affect their lives just like adults. You may be able to provide contextual information that may help to provide a deeper understanding of the children you teach. Do not take offence when your headteacher is disappointed in the progress of a child and remember that they are ultimately responsible for all the children in the school. If a child has not made expected progress, think about what could be done to help the child in the future. Have a discussion and try to alter your practice accordingly. Again, this demonstrates a willingness to be open and to continue to be a learner. Your headteacher should be impressed that you present in this way as they will know that you have the right mind set to continue to develop as a teacher. This piece of advice is exactly the same for observations. Learn from them, speak up when you know you have made mistakes, and most certainly celebrate your achievements. Your headteacher will never expect you to be perfect but they will expect you to be open to learning.

Mentor

Your mentor must be someone that is approachable and who you see on a fairly regular basis; someone who you can be open and honest with. This person is probably part of senior leadership so their time will be precious. Make sure you value their time and input by always being on time and prepared for meetings. Come to meetings with 1 or 2 key points that you would like to discuss or some key questions and show that you have been proactive, where possible, in seeking out potential solutions. Be honest and say when you are finding things hard. If your last observation of a phonics lesson had some key areas for improvement, ask if you can be released to watch 10 minutes of an experienced teacher's lesson. Being proactive in this way will demonstrate to your mentor that you are thinking about and taking some ownership of your practice. Asking to go on a course or a whole hour out of the classroom may be too much, but 10 minutes is usually achievable.

When you write your first ever report, show it to your mentor and get feedback to ensure you are on the right track. This should ensure that your time is used well and you should be on track from the start, rather than facing a massive re-write.

For this relationship to work it must be two way. You are the key person teaching your class and your mentor is the person that is helping you to become a better teacher. They can feed you with invaluable professional help and advice but ultimately you are the person who needs to put that advice into practice; they cannot do it for you. Sometimes your mentor might have to be really straight talking and honest with you and you might not always like what you hear. This is when you need to understand that they are only doing their best to help you to improve and you must not take it personally. It is a professional relationship. Absolutely every teacher will have key points for improvements and even headteachers usually have their own mentors. The teacher/mentor relationship is one in which respect for each other should be reciprocal.

Key points for being a good mentee

	Tick
I am: ■ on time and prepare for my mentor meetings;	
■ honest and open with my mentor;	
■ proactive in seeking help;	
■ good at taking on board advice and putting it into practice;	
■ good at acknowledging positive feedback.	
I always thank my mentor.	

Office staff, lunchtime supervisors, cleaners, and site manager

These people are absolutely key members of staff and should be treated as such. Building up excellent relationships with all these people will make for a positive working environment. You also need to ensure that the children treat all people in the school with respect. Children need to be taught, for example, that tidying the classroom before the cleaner comes in is really important, or making sure that waste at lunchtime is cleared away properly. If you have had a particularly messy art session, do apologise to the cleaner and say you will make sure the children empty the dirty water more carefully next time.

The start of the afternoon session should have a routine just like the morning and the end of the day, so that if a lunchtime supervisor wants a word with you, they are able to. Having a small window of time to sort out any lunchtime disputes or upsets will help children settle for an afternoon of learning. It is also important that the lunchtime supervisors know that their feedback is valuable.

Showing respect for all who work in the community of the school is key to building a community where all help each other. This community is like a big jigsaw where all the pieces are crucial. Looking after each other with common courtesies on a daily basis, and occasionally asking about how things are, will help you to know more about these people and, as a result, you will be able to develop these relationships.

Asking the site manager or lunchtime supervisors, for example, if they would like to come to your class assembly would be a lovely way of demonstrating that you value their presence. Making thank you cards for these key people at the end of an academic year or even termly will be really appreciated and as a result these people will often go the extra mile for you.

Summary

Relationships in the community of a school are multi-layered and each layer needs to be understood and nurtured. I was asked recently what you should do as a teacher if no one in the school really respects each other and if the culture is predominantly one of gossip. It is simple; no matter how hard it is, you need to be the shining light. Model to others kindness, like making a cup of tea for someone, and simply do not get involved when unnecessary staffroom gossip occurs. A small light can be seen from a distance and can grow. You can be that light. Most people within a school value each other highly and understand that each individual has a part to play in making the school a community where staff and pupils are continually learning academically, socially, emotionally, and sometimes spiritually. Positive working relationships are the firm foundations that allow everyone to achieve their best.

Check list

	Tick
I have routines at the beginning and end of the day so that I am able to speak to parents/carers if necessary;	
I am: ◦ mindful of strategies of how to speak to parents about their child or deal with a 'tricky' situation	
◦ a good mentee (look at mentee checklist).	
I take: ◦ time to prepare for parent/carer consultations	
◦ on board advice and demonstrate I am part of a team;	
I ensure TAs/LSAs are fully informed of planning and know their role within a lesson.	
I demonstrate that I value all staff in the community of school.	

CHAPTER

14

Looking after yourself

This chapter should help you to:

- understand the importance of looking ahead and being prepared;
- understand how you can help yourself on a daily basis;
- look after yourself and be resilient;
- look to the future.

Introduction

In my research for this book, one of the key pieces of advice that NQT mentors have given me is the need for NQTs to pace themselves throughout the year. Indeed, pacing yourself, good use of time, looking after yourself, and resilience are all key to ensuring that teachers stay in the profession. As well as planning for the teaching and learning of the children, you need to ensure that you plan for your well-being.

Looking ahead and being prepared

I would strongly advise making a termly timeline of key events that will affect you during each term. These are events that you will not necessarily have planned for as a trainee teacher and you may not necessarily be aware of, so it would be beneficial to ask your mentor to help you plot this timeline. Knowing what will be happening in advance should help you to prepare and feel more settled and in control. Here are examples of how you might plan in advance.

Example of an Autumn 1st half term timeline plotting key events

Week 1	Week 2	Week 3	Week 4	Week 5	Week 6	Week 7
Meeting with mentor		SEN(D) target setting	Lesson observation headteacher	Meeting with mentor		Class assembly

Key points:
Week 1

- At the first meeting with your mentor ensure that you have all relevant data on your class and really importantly, the implications of this data for teaching and learning.

Week 2

- You should be aware of the previous targets for any children with special needs in your class. Be extra mindful when teaching these children in week 2 so that you can feel more confident providing any relevant information at the target setting meeting with the SENCO/Inclusion manager in week 3. Your TA/LSA should be able to help you gather information on these children.

Week 3, 4, and 5

- Prepare your lesson that will be observed by the headteacher by the end of week 3 so that you will not be worrying about it over the weekend. This will also give you time to talk through the lesson with your mentor.
- The feedback from the headteacher's observation should feed into the discussion at the meeting with your mentor. Remember feedback is different to criticism. Note any positive feedback.

Week 6

- The material for the class assembly should come from learning that naturally occurs in the half term (see Chapter 9). Make sure you have a couple of rehearsals in the hall in week 6. You will need to think about ensuring these slots are available in advance. Remember that a class assembly is not a full blown West End production!

Example of an Autumn 2nd half term timeline plotting key events

Week 1	Week 2	Week 3	Week 4	Week 5	Week 6	Week 7
Meeting with mentor	Assessment week	Parent/carer consultations		Lesson observation Headteacher Christmas Fayre	Christmas concert	Meeting with mentor

Key points:
Week 1

- Ensure you know exactly what will be happening in assessment week in the meeting with your mentor.
- If necessary, ensure that children are prepared for assessments, which may mean revision of key learning which will affect weekly and daily planning.
- Material for the Christmas concert should be started here as part of lessons (see Chapter 9).

Week 2

- Mark any assessments straight away so that they can feed into parent/carer consultations.
- In preparation for parent/carer consultations, collect some key information from the children, such as:
  - their favourite subject;
  - what they find particularly challenging in Mathematics and English;
  - what would help them in their learning;
  - what they love doing out of school.

This knowledge is always helpful in demonstrating that you really know the children.

- Ensure you can talk with confidence about every child's progress in Mathematics and English as well as key targets. You might want the children to mark in their books something they are really proud of achieving so that you can show the parents/carers. All of this takes time.
- By the end of the week all books should be marked and up to date ready for parent/carer consultations. You may want to consider the amount of recording in books immediately prior to the consultations so that you can manage everything.

Week 3

- The morning after parent/carer consultations, ensure the children have learning that is not too taxing and try to ensure minimum marking as you will be tired.
- Plan for when you can have the hall for rehearsals for the Christmas concert.
- Ensure anything your class needs to prepare for the Christmas Fayre is completed this week.

Week 4

- At the end of week 4, you should be prepared for your lesson observation by the headteacher.

Week 5

- Ensure all costumes/scenery for the Christmas concert are in place.
- In the final 3 weeks of term, keep routines and teaching as per usual.

The Christmas Fayre should not be an issue if you have planned in advance for anything that needs to be prepared by your class. Similarly, if the material for the Christmas concert has been mainly taught as part of lessons, this should reduce stress for both yourself and the children.

Week 7

In preparation for your mentor meeting reflect on your first term and write down:

- 2 aspects of your practice you have improved;
- 2 aspects of your practice that you are doing really well;
- 2 key targets for improvement next term.

This preparation should only take 5 minutes but will demonstrate that you are prepared for your meeting. It should also help you to get things in perspective and make you acknowledge what you have achieved. Also, 2 or 3 targets is enough to concentrate on, so do not overload yourself with any more.

I cannot emphasise enough the importance of keeping teaching and routines right until the end of term where you possibly can. Calm, quiet lessons are needed when they are interspersed with concerts, parties, and a general sense of end of term excitement filtering through the school. Staff become tired and children also become tired, so a quiet and calm approach to everything can really help.

Pace yourself . . . look ahead and be prepared.

My advice would be for you to plan for every term in the same way as I have demonstrated earlier so that you can pace yourself. Each 'new event' will be so much easier to manage if you are well prepared. This should mean that you are less likely to be reactive and more likely to make considered decisions. Planning in this way helps you to look forward as opposed to always being 'in the moment'.

There are certain points in the year when pacing yourself is particularly important, such as report writing time. If you are in a school where the tradition is to send out end of year reports, it will be key to prepare carefully in advance. Just after Easter time, meet with your mentor and organise the best way to prepare. Looking at excellent examples can help, as can carefully pacing yourself, completing a few a week or a subject at a time. Ask your mentor to check the quality of your report writing early on so that you can adjust your writing accordingly.

How can I help myself on a daily basis?

Understanding how to help yourself on a daily basis is really important. Addressing certain aspects of practice can make all the difference to your well-being and to your resilience. So here are some things to think about that should help you.

Low level disruption

The importance of classroom rules has been addressed in this book. It is the continual use of these rules that must be addressed throughout the whole year. The 'pinch points' can come just before a holiday when you are likely to be tired and let things slip. Also, after a holiday, it can become evident in the behaviour of the children that the rules and routines need to be reinforced again. This happens to most teachers; refresh and remind the children and make sure you reinforce them. Do not be afraid to take time highlighting your clear expectations. Be consistent.

Marking

Having piles of books to mark at the end of the day can be so time consuming. Also, you have to ask yourself whether you really have the time to mark all the books well every day and whether there will be a real impact on learning. Try to:

- mark as much as you can with the children;
- get the children to mark some of their work;
- include peer marking in lessons.

Sticking in sheets of paper

You cannot afford to spend time sticking sheets and sheets of paper into books. Model to the children how this should be done at the beginning of the year. It is not the end of the world if sheets are not completely straight.

Tidying the classroom

The children should tidy the classroom. Make sure the classroom is tidy and ready for the next session before the children go to playtime or to lunch. Before the end of the day, get all the children's books, bags, homework, coats, letters, and lunch boxes ready on their tables before you settle down to a calm story, song, or reflective time at the end of the day. When absolutely everything is tidied away the children can have a lovely 15-minute end of day session with you.

Sorting out disputes

Sorting out playtime or lunchtime disputes can be time consuming. It may be worth having a routine for the start of every afternoon that allows the children to engage in a learning activity that does not require your input. This will free you up to sort out any problems. The dispute may have to be sorted out at the next break time; it is no surprise that this usually helps to sort out disputes more quickly. Remember that you are teaching children how to behave; this is part of the role of a teacher. Embrace it and congratulate yourself when behaviour improves.

Social media

WhatsApp groups or other similar groups may be created for teachers in a year group or Key Stage. Whilst this form of communication can be very useful, you cannot be expected to be on call at all times. I would suggest you should be on call from 8 in the morning to 6 o'clock in the evening, unless it is a real emergency. Make sure work emails are not on your phone and that you make a clear distinction between work and home time. Consider disabling/switching off messages/email alerts so that you are actively choosing when to check things.

Low level staff disputes in school

Keep out of any negative conversations that can occur. Someone once told me that when others are negative, think of yourself in a bubble; the negative energy of others just bounces off you and cannot penetrate the bubble. This really helped me.

Do not feel guilty

When you leave at 6 o'clock to go to your choir rehearsal, do not feel guilty when a member of staff tells you that they have not got time to do anything other than schoolwork in the evenings. Switching off will be so good for you.

Being physically active and reflective with your class

Make physical exercise part of every day with your class; 10 minutes can be spent on a school jog or movement to music or whatever you and your children will benefit from or enjoy most. The children can encourage you and you can encourage the children to get fitter. Also spend time as a class listening to a piece of music or an uplifting piece of writing or poem. Children (and staff) can find it hard to 'just be' and listen. The children may be giggly at first, but over time it can be a really peaceful and reflective time.

Looking after yourself and being resilient

Teaching is like a marathon and not a sprint. You need to pace yourself and look after yourself every step of the way. You need to make sure that when there is the possibility of 'hitting the wall' you plan accordingly. Try to:

- aim to make most of your working days from 8 until 6 o'clock;
- target what you realistically want to achieve by the end of the working day and tick these tasks off your list;
- plan carefully for an 'easier' day after the occasional evening when you need to work late;
- set up your class for the next day before you leave school;
- deploy your TA/LSA effectively.

I always tried to make sure that I worked really hard between the hours of 8 and 6 and yes, of course, I had some evenings when I worked particularly late. Getting on with things and completing jobs stopped the worry of thinking about what I needed to do. You must be mindful that it is so easy for teaching to take over your life and you can start to say to friends that you cannot go out because of the amount of work you have to do. Someone gave me a piece of advice when I started teaching that if teaching becomes your life how can you teach children about life if you are not experiencing it yourself? You must make sure that you look after yourself and have a life outside school. It is absolutely crucial that you make sure you have other interests such as keeping fit, being a member of a choir or a book club. Switching off from the needs of the children in your class can be hard but crucial to ensuring that you keep everything in perspective and that you are fresh and ready to teach them in the morning. Ultimately, this will help the children you teach. Engaging in a hobby of your own will help you to switch off, relax, and then probably sleep better. It is very hard to talk about teaching when you are singing or dancing to music!

Getting a good night's sleep is key to your well-being and resilience so make sure you have routines in the evening that will help you to relax. Switch off electronic devices and keep phones and laptops out of the bedroom. Think of your bedroom as a place to recharge yourself. Think of yourself in a bubble where only positive thoughts can filter through.

'Me time' makes me a better teacher.

Whatever happens, do not lose sight of your well-being as this will help your resilience throughout the term. Planning for your well-being is important. If you followed the advice in the first part of this book, you will be aware of the importance of key elements that can help your well-being. Reflect on how well you are doing and re-set yourself every term so that you do not lose sight of your own needs.

Key elements to help well-being are:	Ideas
connecting with others;	■ Greet people every morning and say your farewells at the end of the day. ■ Go to the staff room for at least 20 minutes at lunchtime and have your lunch with others. ■ Stop to have a cup of tea with others at the end of the school day. ■ Meet up with friends from outside school every week.
learning from others;	■ Ask for advice when necessary. ■ Learn from others around you and tell them you are learning from them. ■ Learn something that has nothing to do with teaching.
being active;	■ Try to be active every day. Can you walk all or part of the way to school? Can you join in with the daily class jog? Can you attend a keep fit class on the way home from school? Can a keep fit class for staff be run in the school?
helping others;	■ Offer help to someone else in the school at least once every week (making a cup of tea, getting their resources when you are collecting yours).
looking after yourself.	■ At the beginning of every half term book yourself a treat (massage, facial, concert). ■ Celebrate your successes with a treat. ■ Use your time in school well so that there is time for you after the school day is completed.

The right mind set

I have taught a few trainee teachers who I thought would make excellent teachers, however, they found teaching to be highly stressful. What they found particularly difficult was the fact that they were perfectionists and wanted to do everything right and get absolutely everything done. In teaching, there is always something more you could do and always something that you could be doing better. Rather than finding this stressful, you need to be able to see it as a positive of the job; you should never be bored, as there is always so much to learn.

You need to embrace advice and targets. If you see yourself as someone who is constantly evolving, changing, and improving, you should be a much happier teacher. You have to be kind to yourself and be realistic about what you can change or improve every term. Most of us can cope with no more than 3 realistic, timebound targets at a time. You should also hear all the positive comments given to you; make sure you write them down and look at them.

Advice and targets are not criticism.

The political nature of education ensures that the goal posts are always changing and new ideas are always being presented. Whatever external pressures there are, or whatever new terms are being used, the teacher is the key element in the classroom that has the potential to impact on the progress of the children in their care. The language of education might change but the core elements of what makes a good teacher never really change that much. As you become more experienced, you will begin to make subtle changes to your practice that enable you to become more proficient at this highly skilful job. Remember that we all make mistakes; I have made many. The key thing is to learn from them and move on.

Looking to the future

Teaching has the potential to be the most amazing job if you have the right skills, are in the right school, are supported well, and actually enjoy what you are doing. Occasionally teachers may find themselves in schools that do not really suit them or meet their needs. My advice in this situation would be to learn from your experience and move on to a school that you choose really carefully and one in which you will be well supported.

If you are settled in the school in which you are teaching, it would be really helpful if you could teach in the same year group again the following academic year, as you will have all the planning in place and can learn from your successes as well as from your mistakes. Also, you are less likely to have to move classrooms. Your second year of teaching should be a year of consolidation. You may have had a highly successful first year and your headteacher might offer you more responsibility. Be careful that the floodgates do not suddenly open and you take on too much. Be honest about what is manageable whilst making sure you do contribute to the life of the school. Often, and especially in single form entry schools, most members of staff have to take on board some responsibility but you will need to know exactly what this entails. Sometimes it is useful to shadow a more experienced member of staff or go on some courses to deepen your understanding of a particular area of the curriculum. You may want to undertake a Master's degree, whereby you can study an aspect of a subject or pedagogy in depth. The studying could have the potential to feed into your personal development as well as impact on the development of the school. This will be a discussion to have with your headteacher and mentor. This may be just what you need or you may feel that concentrating on your teaching is more than enough. Year on year, evaluate what you personally need. Make sure that you think carefully about your own development in the profession and do not be afraid to keep your own personal goals in sight.

Successful teachers are often given the more challenging classes in a school, as well as extra responsibilities. When this happens year on year, teachers may become overloaded. If this becomes the case for you, do not be afraid to have open and honest conversations about what is achievable and how you are feeling. Teachers are more likely to stay in the profession if the workload is manageable and they feel valued.

> *Look after yourself so that you will be able to look after the children you teach.*

Final word

Dear reader, I have been in a privileged position in my career where I have been able to visit many schools and work alongside talented teachers. Some of these teachers have been quiet and unassuming and others have been full of life and bubbly. Whatever character traits they have, they are able to engage with children who want to be taught by them. They are quietly confident in their own abilities but always with an understanding that they are learners themselves and always will be. They are unfazed by the different characters that make up the 'rich tapestry' of school life and have the personal skills to deal with a plethora of situations. They empathise but are strong in their values and beliefs and hold true to them when necessary. They are usually highly organised and can therefore manage change well. They are also able to enjoy 'being in the moment' with the children they teach as well as working out the intricate puzzle of helping some children to access learning. Watch these people, talk to them, and learn from them. You will undoubtedly discover that these teachers have had the same insecurities and worries as any newly qualified teacher and that they also still face challenges from time to time.

Think about an experienced teacher as an experienced mountaineer.

Experienced mountaineers have the kit. Their shoes have been broken in and are comfortable. They know what to do at different points in the climb because they've done it before and they rely on others at tricky points. Very occasionally they lose their footing but the team helps them. They pace themselves because they know what is coming next. They look for new routes and challenges.

Think about a newly qualified teacher as an inexperienced mountaineer.

The inexperienced mountaineer doesn't have all the kit but they learn what they need over time. Their shoes have not been broken in, so sometimes their feet hurt a little to start with but this gets better over time. Not knowing the mountain they are climbing is daunting at first but this gets easier as they get to know the terrain and know who to ask for help. They sometimes lose their footing but the team help them get back on track. They learn that planning for the journey ahead and pacing themselves helps.

I sincerely hope that this book helps you on your journey.
Bronwen Cullum